50 HIKES
IN
ARIZONA

By James R. Mitchell

50 HIKES IN ARIZONA

First Edition, August 1973
Second Edition, October 1973
Third Edition, July 1976
Fourth Edition, January 1979
Fifth Edition, September 1985
Sixth Edition, January 1991

Manufactured in the U.S.A.

**Published by
Gem Guides Book Co.
315 Cloverleaf Dr., Suite F
Baldwin Park, California 91706**

ISBN 0-935182-47-0
Library of Congress Catalog Card No. 91-070049

Note: Due to the possibility of personal error, typographical error, misinterpretation of information, and the many changes both natural and man-made, **50 Hikes in Arizona,** its author, publisher and all other persons directly and indirectly associated with this publication assume no responsibility for accidents, injury or any losses by individuals or groups using this publication.

In rough terrain and hazardous areas all persons are advised to be aware of possible changes due to the elements or those hazards which may be man made that can occur along any of the hiking trails.

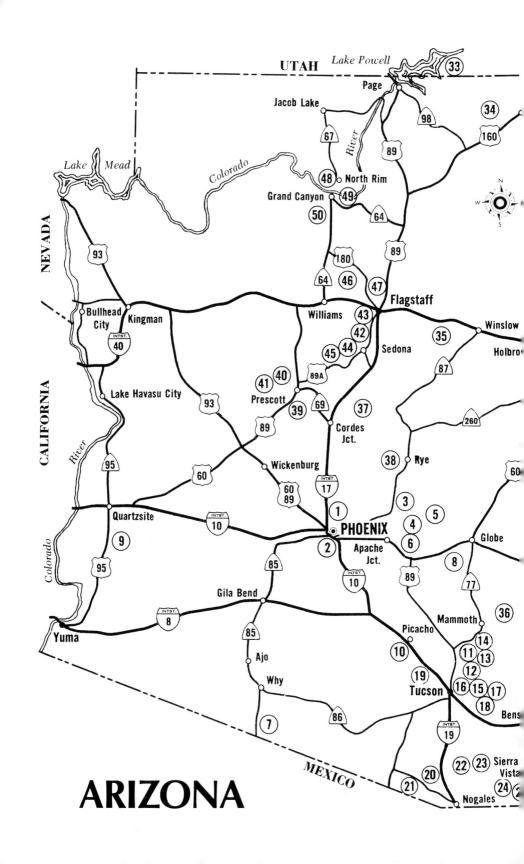

ARIZONA

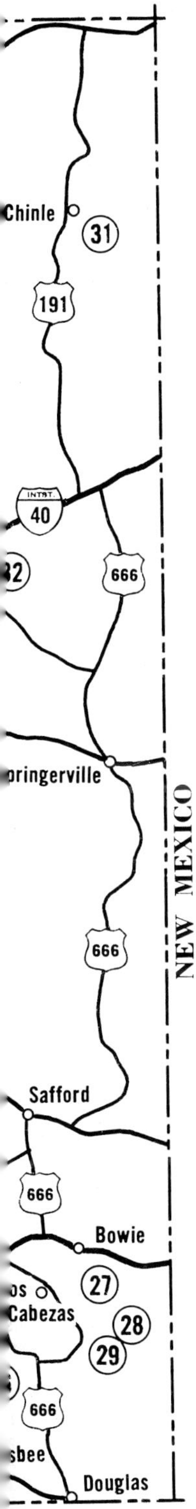

Chinle
31
191
INTST 40
42
666
666
NEW MEXICO
oringerville
666
Safford
666
Bowie
os
Cabezas
27
28
29
666
sbee
Douglas

Sedona/Oak Creek Canyon Area

INTRODUCTION

Few states can compare with Arizona when it comes to contrasting hiking environments. Its climate ranges from hot Sonoran desert to alpine conditions above timberline and includes almost everything between. There are rolling grasslands dotted with prickle poppies and desert-willows; red sandstone cliffs streaked with desert varnish; eroded volcanic cones and craggy peaks; sunny woodlands dominated by oaks, pines and junipers; solemn forests of spruce and fir; and there is the desert where elusive tanks and tinajas dole out water in some of its most beautiful forms.

These habitats account for a wide variety of birds, mammals, insects and plants, many of which are curiously adapted to their environments. So many habitats also provide endless variations of landscapes and terrains ideally suited to hiking.

We have tried to describe hikes which give access to a cross-section of Arizona's best scenery. The Bright Angel is America's most famous hiking trail, dropping from the pine-clad south rim of the Grand Canyon to the Colorado River 4,500 feet below. There are desert hikes such as South Mountain Park near Phoenix and Wasson Peak near Tucson; there are hikes in the cool pines around Prescott and Sedona. For the history buff there are hikes to Indian dwellings such as White House Ruins and Keet Seel and a hike to old Fort Bowie.

The hikes vary in length from one mile to twenty-eight miles round trip. Some are well marked; some are not marked at all. Keep in mind that the distance you cover is not so important as what you see and learn. Our best memories are not of arrivals and departures but of sunsets, elf owls, wildflowers and windmills.

The original fifty hikes were published in 1972-1973. We have tried to keep the book as current as possible by revising it in 1976, in 1978, and again in 1985. In the process, more than half the trails and routes have been completely re-hiked. Almost all trailheads have been driven to at least twice. Concerned government agencies have been consulted throughout.

Keep in mind that all descriptions are general. Despite our best efforts, there will be discrepancies. A trail may be washed out by summer rains, cattle may indulge in some "creative trail building," short-cut trails and trails of use may develop, trail crews may relocate part of a trail—the possibilities are too numerous to mention.

On many of the hikes it will be necessary to stop and look for the route. We have tried to go into extra detail where an area seemed confusing to us, however (due to changes or to luck), you may have difficulty where we had none. In the field, the final responsibility for finding and following the route has to lie with the hiker whose footsteps must be guided by common sense.

HOW TO USE THIS BOOK

This book is merely a guide, to be used in conjunction with your own intellect and abilities. Our intention is to suggest possible outings which we ourselves have enjoyed. To provide more than general descriptions would require a volume ten times this size (and price), so it is up to you, the hiker, to find and follow the various routes.

If you lose a trail or are not certain of the route, **always** consider returning to the trailhead rather than risk getting lost. Experience will gradually make you proficient at route finding; however, even veteran hikers must occasionally admit defeat.

Most hikes include alternate routes and most all contain information on side trips that can be made from that particular area. The information given in this book will yield much more than 50 hikes throughout the national parks and all areas covered in the state. Those who hike one trail will want to come back to try that alternate route or side trip that was passed up on the first hike because of lack of time or preparation.

All road and trail mileages are approximate. Road mileages were calculated using a truck odometer, but odometer readings will vary in different vehicles. If the description indicates a distance of nine miles to a trailhead, start watching for it as you approach that mileage, but don't expect it to come up exactly on the ninth mile.

Trail mileages have been taken from various sources of information including maps and signs. Where no other information was available, estimates were used. On any hikes re-done since 1976, a measuring wheel was used which increased our accuracy. Don't rely too heavily on trail signs; some may not be accurate, and many are just plain missing.

If you are a novice hiker, start with short outings and work your way up to the longer treks. The times given for the various hikes are only approximate, and slower hikers may need considerably more time than indicated. There is no particular accomplishment in covering twenty or thirty miles in a day anyway. There are thousands of people who can do this, including some children. You'll get more memories to the mile if you take time to observe and interpret what you see.

If you have only a few hours to spare, consider taking one of the shorter hikes or limiting yourself to the first part of a longer hike. On the other hand, if you're looking for a week of solitude, it's here in exchange for a little planning and hiking.

Study our section on precautions, and add to it from your own experience and other sources of information. Keep the statistics boring by not becoming one of them.

DIFFERENT REGIONS

There is a tremendous variation from one area of Arizona to another and from one altitude to the next. Although it is difficult to generalize, as you travel around the state, you will notice that certain patterns of plants and associated animals keep repeating themselves. These associations are called "communities." With a little practice, you will have no difficulty in recognizing the major communities. We recommend that you obtain some field guides to plants and animals and learn as you hike. This is a painless way to increase your knowledge and enhances your hike as well.

DESERT COMMUNITIES: Much of southern and western Arizona is very hot and dry. You will find that there are actually several types of desert communities, each with many differences and similarities. The creosotebush community and the saguaro-palo verde community are the most common of the desert communities. Cacti are abundant; and lizards, insects, snakes and certain mammals have all evolved adaptations which enable them to survive under these harsh conditions. The kangaroo rat and round-tailed ground squirrel fit this category. There is considerable variation in desert terrain--some is very flat and stretches for seemingly empty miles; other areas are steep and rocky. Some of the hikes which are in desert communities are South Mountain Park, Bull Pasture and Pima Canyon.

GRASSLAND COMMUNITIES: In the southeastern part of the state and in scattered other areas, there are places where grasses and yuccas dominate the landscape. Antelope once roamed here, but deer and jackrabbits are still common. Your hikes to Atascosa Lookout and Coronado Peak will afford some fine views of grassland communities.

WOODLAND COMMUNITIES: Depending on your location, there are several somewhat distinct types of communities which fit into this group. One community of the woodland type is dominated by oaks, another by mixed oaks and pines, and still another by pinyon pines and junipers. To us, Mexican jays seem to be one of the most typical animals found in this community. Many of the hikes pass through this type of area, in part at least. Included are Tortilla Ranch, Cochise Stronghold, Fort Bowie and Chiricahua National Monument.

CONIFEROUS FOREST COMMUNITIES: Large stands of ponderosa pines are common in many areas of Arizona, while Douglas fir and Engelmann spruce are more common in others. A few black bear still inhabit these forests, and Steller's jays are common. Aspen Trail and the Kendrick Peak hike will take you through fine examples of this type of community.

ALPINE-TUNDRA COMMUNITY: Arizona's only example of this type of community is a small area above timberline in the San Francisco Peaks near Flagstaff. Vegetation grows close to the ground, summers are very short, and snow often remains on the ground well into July. Winter conditions are severe. The hike to the summit of Mount Humphreys is the only trip into this type of community. Stick to established routes as the alpine vegetation is very sensitive. The harsh environment and short growing season severely limit a plant's ability to recover from trampling.

LIFE ZONES: In Arizona, you can start hiking in a desert community where cacti are common and temperatures high, head up a mountain and pass through examples of grassland communities, woodland communities and coniferous forest communities. As the elevation increases, the average temperature decreases, and the amount of precipitation increases. The different communities you pass through are often called "life zones." In other words, life zones are simply different communities arranged vertically. You may hear of the Lower Sonoran Life Zone (sea level to 4,000 feet, depending on location) which includes the desert communities; the Upper Sonoran Life Zone (3,500 to 7,000 feet) which includes the grassland and woodland communities; the Transition Life Zone (6,000 to 9,000 feet) which includes the ponderosa pine part of the coniferous forest communities; the Canadian Life Zone (8,000 to 10,000 feet) which includes the Douglas fir part of the coniferous forest communities; and the Hudsonian Life Zone which includes the Engelmann spruce part of the coniferous forest communities. At the top of Mount Humphreys is the Arctic-Alpine Life Zone (11,500 to 12,670 feet).

LET'S SAVE SOMETHING

This section of our book used to be titled "Let's Save Arizona." We now realize that it is too late for that. Arizonans used to shake their heads and deplore the smog and traffic in southern California. Now Arizona has become the darling of the sunbelt, and with popularity came crowding and the desert's equivalent to smog, "smust." To the chronic problems of mining development and smelter smoke have been added vehicular emissions, urban sprawl and a sinking water table. Arizona is being bulldozed away by developers who, for a price, could have built into the existing landscape without stripping the vegetation and evicting the wildlife. Growth could have been planned and contained. The chambers of commerce have successfully wooed eastern industries which are establishing large plants and employing thousands. One can now see a good ballet in Arizona, but many of us would rather have seen blue sky. So it goes.

Still, if you're buying our books, you must have some interest in the outdoors. If you're new to the state or a novice to hiking, we hope you will learn to respect the land and its animals and do your part to preserve some of what's left. We have mixed emotions about selling a book which brings people into the backcountry; yet we know that if

we didn't, someone else would who might unduly publicize delicate areas or rare animals. We try to describe hikes into country that will entice you to get out more and inspire you to protect it. If you do much hiking, you are eventually going to stumble upon the rare animals and delicate environments and, hopefully, cherish them as we do. Perhaps you'll care enough to write letters to your legislators when a special area is threatened. We can only hope that while our books increase backcountry use they will also increase the numbers of people who appreciate it and wish to preserve it.

Motorcycles, dunebuggies and four-wheel-drive vehicles are probably doing more damage to the Arizona landscape than all other sources combined. One look at the foothills and creekbeds near any major city will graphically illustrate the need for laws prohibiting off-road travel by vehicles. The laws must be enacted quickly; already the scars will outlast our lifetimes.

The sleepy Southwest of the '40s and '50s is gone, but there is a lot of beautiful country left in Arizona. Do what you can to prevent unnecessary destruction, and see it while you can--it may be under cement tomorrow.

SEASONS AND WATER

The seasonal status of the various hikes should be considered approximate as climates and conditions vary from one year to the next. Consider early or late snowstorms, snowcover, rain, high water, etc., in planning an outing. If in doubt, a call to the appropriate local government agency may be of some help.

Arizona is very hot in summer. We cannot recommend desert hikes at this time although the trails are not closed unless there is fire danger. We have rated all hikes which are below 3,000 feet as being "hot in summer." This usually means temperatures in excess of a hundred degress Fahrenheit. We normally would not hike at this time of year, and few local people do. Your body requires water in quantities that may be impractical to carry--and we recommend that you start out with all the water you anticipate needing. Even for a two-mile outing, a gallon of water per person would not be too much.

It is not unusual for an entire national forest to be closed for short periods during the year when there is high fire danger. No hiking is permitted at these times, so check with the appropriate government agency if in doubt.

MAPS

Our maps have been drawn from a variety of sources and are intended only to show the general layout of the hike. They are not drawn to scale, and the directional arrow is approximate. The main route is indicated by dashed lines; side trails and other trails are indicated by dotted lines.

U.S. Geological Survey topographic maps are available for all of the hikes except Keet Seel. They are very useful for showing topographic features, and we strongly recommend their use. Keep in mind that some of the details, especially on older maps, may be outdated. The names of the appropriate topographic maps have been included on our drawn maps. "Topo" maps are available at many local outlets or from the U.S. Geological Survey (see address under "Government Agencies").

PRECAUTIONS

All trails and routes described in this book undoubtedly have many potential hazards. While there is always the possibility of unforseen trouble to which no one is immune, most problems can be avoided through preparation and caution. The following list is intended to get you thinking and is by no means complete. We do not have room to go into every conceivable problem, medical or otherwise, that you might encounter on these hikes. We're just anxious to make you aware of some of the most common hazards to be prepared for or--better yet--avoided. Study each item carefully, and apply it to your own situation. We strongly recommend that you obtain a copy of the book, DESERT SURVIVAL, which discusses many of these subjects in detail.

(1) Unless you're planning a very long trip, carry all the water you anticipate using. If you must rely on one or more supplemental sources of water, ascertain that they are active and potable **before** you set out. There are a number of springs marked on the various topo maps listed for each trail, but some may be seasonal or badly polluted. Some may

have been dry for years. Even on a cool summer day, one gallon of water per person should be considered an absolute minimum in the desert. There have been numerous occasions when we drank more than two gallons apiece. All water should be treated with water purification tablets if it comes from a source along the hike.

(2) Take an American Red Cross first-aid course, and carry a complete first-aid kit. Because many of the hikes in this book are in hot climates, be familiar with the first aid for heat cramps, heat exhaustion and heat stroke. Better yet, know how to prevent them in the first place. Always carry salt, and be sure your body is getting enough water and salt in hot weather.

(3) Stay on established trails or routes. If you lose a trail, don't hesitate to turn around and return to the trailhead--you can fortify yourself with information from a local ranger district or a veteran hiker and tackle the hike another day. Many of the fatal accidents that have occurred over the years in Arizona were the result of hikers leaving trails, taking short-cuts or climbing cliffs. (The rock on many of Arizona's mountains is unstable and not suitable for climbing.)

(4) Always carry matches in a waterproof container and a flashlight with spare bulb and batteries. Be prepared to spend the night out even if you only plan a dayhike.

(5) Many hikers prefer solo hiking, and it offers some advantages such as the likelihood of seeing more wildlife and setting your own pace. The basic problem with hiking alone is that even a minor injury such as a sprained ankle could be serious if it occurred in an isolated area. Without anyone to go for help, it could be days or weeks before help happened along. If you do hike alone, be sure to let someone know of your intentions and itinerary.

(6) Be careful around cacti and agaves. Both jumping cholla and teddy bear cholla are common in many of the desert areas described in this book. A deeply imbedded stem can be a serious problem and may require pliers for removal. A lightly imbedded stem can be flipped off by using a pocket comb.

(7) Be alert. Eleven species of rattlesnakes occur in Arizona, although some are rather restricted in their ranges. If you do much hiking in the state, you

will eventually see one. Don't carry a handgun for the purpose of murdering snakes--just walk around them. They are preoccupied with their own affairs which do not include the intentional pursuit of hikers. (If that were the case, we can think of several authors who would be writing cookbooks instead of hiking guides.) Be careful not to threaten; snakes are fearful of being stepped on, reached for, shot at or sat upon--and if retreat seems to be cut off, they will resort to their only other defense. Most snakebites occur when someone is careless or attempts to capture or handle a snake.

You might encounter an Arizona coral snake on some rare occasion, but they are not a threat unless you attempt to handle them. We have occasionally seen Gila monsters. These plump, beaded, lethargic lizards are of great interest and are not dangerous unless crowded or handled--at which time they can become surprisingly animated.

(8) Wear appropriate clothing and footgear. In hot weather, avoid exposing your skin to the direct sun. Wear a long-sleeved shirt, a wide-brimmed hat that protects the back of your neck, and denim pants (not cut-offs). Carry extra clothing in your pack in case the weather should change suddenly. Be sure footgear is thoroughly broken in. (Blisters are one of the hiker's most common problems.)

(9) Plan your trips carefully during the summer monsoon season. Don't camp in washes or other areas subject to flash flooding. Some normally dry washes can quickly become raging torrents, making crossing impossible for a few hours to several days depending on the severity of the storm.

(10) Lightning is a potential threat, particularly during the summer monsoon season. Avoid prominence when selecting a campsite or when waiting out a storm. Remember that a direct hit is not necessary for a lightning strike to be fatal; the charge has a tendency to spread out on the surface and to travel in all directions.

(11) The bark scorpion, the black widow spider and other species of biting or stinging arthropods are fairly common in places, rare in others. Don't pick up a rock or stick without checking the underside. Make sure clothing and boots are uninhabited before putting them on.

In certain areas there may be several species of small flies which can make hiking and camping miserable, especially during the spring. Have head and neck protection and a long-sleeved shirt. Be sure to carry some effective insect repellent to protect exposed skin. Use an insect-proof tent.

(12) Many areas of Arizona are subject to cold weather. In some parts of the state, winter temperatures may fall many degrees below zero degrees Fahrenheit. Some trails and routes described in this book (Mount Humphreys for instance) are not passable in winter by the casual hiker.

Hypothermia is a cooling of the body temperature which, if it progresses too far, can result in death. Common contributing factors are cold temperatures (not necessarily below freezing), wet skin, wet clothing, wind, fatigue and lack of proper nutrients. Be thoroughly familiar with the symptoms of hypothermia and the first-aid treatment of same. Better yet, be prepared to prevent it from occurring.

(13) Exercise regularly and stay in shape, even during times when you aren't planning to hike. Not only does poor conditioning result in a less enjoyable outing, it can also increase the likelihood of other problems.

(14) Keep in mind that the descriptions included here are intended only as a general guide and that trailheads, trail conditions and routes may be subject to change.

EQUIPMENT

Many factors must be considered when selecting equipment. What we take with us depends on the length of the hike, the terrain, the weather and other factors. There are certain basic items which all hikers should consider, and you can add or subtract items from this list to meet your personal needs. We do suggest that you buy quality products that will last.

Emergency kit: We recommend a zippered plastic container in which to carry a wide variety of items for potential use in an emergency. This kit is useful not only on dayhikes and backpacks but in the vehicle as well. Here is a list of items to include in your kit, though you will want to tailor the list to meet your own needs.

Bags (large, plastic-type)
Batteries (extra set for flashlights)
Blanket (emergency-type)
Bulbs (spares for flashlights)
Can opener (small, G.I.-type)
Candies (non-melting)
Compass (quality is important)
Cord (nylon)
Change (for pay phones)
Elastic bandages
Fire starter
First-aid kit (complete enough to meet all
common emergencies)
Flashlights (two small ones per person)
Sun screen
Keys (vehicle—use a safety pin to attach
them to the inside of your pack!)
Knife (pocket-type with a variety of blades)
Insect repellent
Lighter (disposable, butane-type)
Lip salve (sun screen)
Match containers (two, waterproof)
Matches (waterproof)
Moleskin (for prevention or treatment of
blisters)
Money ($20 bill)
Needles and thread
Notebook
Pencil
Prescriptions (extra supply in case of delay)
Razor blade (single-edge in plastic pill
bottle)
Safety pins
Salt tablets
Thermometer (in a case)
Toilet paper
Whistle
Wire

Dayhikes: It is possible to take off for the day with no special equipment, but the outing may be more enjoyable (and you will be in a better position to meet certain emergencies) if at least some items are at hand. Consider taking the following items on all hikes, no matter how short.

(1) A comfortable daypack of light-weight material and good quality. Be sure it is large enough to hold all your gear.

(2) Emergency kit (see description above).

(3) A leak-proof canteen. (Some are made of polyethylene and have an attached cap which cannot be easily lost.)

(4) Enough emergency food, such as non-melting candies and other items, for at least one extra day in the field.

(5) Comfortable, broken-in footwear. High boots might deflect a snakebite, but not always. Be sure footwear is warm

enough for cold weather and that the soles have a good tread.

(6) A thorough knowledge of the currently recommended treatment for snakebite.

(7) Proper clothing. Long pants of a tough fabric help prevent scratches, scrapes and insect bites. In summertime a long-sleeved shirt and a wide-brimmed hat should be worn to protect the skin from exposure to hot sun. In wintertime it may be necessary to carry or wear a down jacket, gloves, hat and long underwear. Winter temperatures often drop well below zero in parts of Arizona.

(8) A rain poncho. Some of those made of newer fabrics "breathe," keeping the rain off but allowing perspiration to evaporate.

(9) Sunglasses to reduce glare and prevent possible sunblindness.

(10) This guide, maps, plant and animal field guides.

(11) Camera with accessories and extra film.

(12) Binoculars.

(13) Toilet paper.

(14) A plastic litter bag.

Backpacks: Hikers of a century ago might have headed out with little more than a bedroll and a minimum amount of food. Living off the land is no longer practical, especially in desert areas. Today's backpacker should bring with him everything he may need and leave no evidence of his visit. This is our list of equipment for a typical backpack.

(1) Everything listed for a dayhike, including the emergency kit, with the exception of the daypack itself.

(2) A comfortably fit backpack of good quality. Most have a waist band which helps to distribute the weight more evenly between the hips and shoulders. Select one large enough to hold everything you need, and consider getting a waterproof cover that will protect the pack and sleeping bag.

(3) A tent will add to the enjoyment of most hikes and, if equipped with a floor and rainfly, can keep you comfortable through a storm. Don't forget the tent poles, tent stakes and whatever cord is necessary to set the tent up.

(4) Your choice of a sleeping bag will depend on the weather. There were summer nights in the bottom of the Grand Canyon when it was so hot that no bag was needed at all. For colder weather, consider goose down—possibly up to three and half pounds

for severe winter conditions. Some people sleep "warm," and some sleep "cold." You will have to experiment to determine your individual needs.

(5) A small portable stove can eliminate the need for a campfire. Fires are prohibited in many areas now because dead wood has been found to be a very important component of ecological systems. There are several excellent, light-weight gas stoves on the market, and they are safe, efficient and clean if used properly.

(6) Many fuel containers have a tendency to leak. Besides making your pack highly aromatic and flammable, a leaky container can ruin your food, so be sure to get one that won't cause problems.

(7) A ground mat is imperative for warmth in cold weather and can also add to the enjoyment of many summer hikes.

(8) Consider the need for fire permits, overnight hiking permits, etc., and have them arranged for in advance if need be.

WALKING TECHNIQUES

Walking for a long distance on a mountain trail with a pack of some sort on your back is quite different from a stroll around the shopping center. The heavy, stiff shoes you wear don't make walking seem any easier either. You will need to develop new walking techniques to conserve your energy and enable you to maintain a good average speed over long distances.

The stiff boots will make you walk flat-footed instead of springing from the toes as many short distance walkers do. Covering a number of miles in a day will require that you maintain a good steady pace, with infrequent rest stops. There will, of course, be times when you will want to stop and look at flora or fauna, or take pictures. If you can't take time to stop and smell the daisies, why bother to hike? But when you are moving, you need to establish a steady pace that you can comfortably maintain for hours. Avoid the rush-ahead and stop-and-rest manner of the inexperienced. Since you will usually be hiking single-file with a group, you must take up the pace of the others, which may be too fast or too slow for you. If you have trouble keeping up, ask the leader to let you set the pace for a while, then go at a speed that is comfortable for you.

Slow down when you go uphill. On very steep trails use the rest step. This requires establishing a slow rhythm. To do the rest step, you straighten and lock the knee on the downhill leg as you move the other foot forward. Pause momentarily, resting your legs, with the uphill knee bent and the weight all supported by the downhill leg. Next shift your weight over the uphill foot, step up on it, straighten the knee and lock it, and advance the other foot, which becomes the uphill foot. Repeat the procedure of straightening and locking the downhill knee and resting the uphill leg. The length of pause between steps depends on factors such as your physical condition, your load, trail steepness, and the altitude. Climbers at very high altitudes may take two or more breaths during each pause between steps.

Some hikers complain that going downhill is more difficult than going uphill, but I remain unconvinced. Going down, take fairly small steps, plant the downhill foot firmly, and shift your weight over it while both feet are solidly on the ground, before taking the next step. Some surfaces are rocky and unstable, and balance is very important. Maintain a comfortable pace downhill and don't let gravity get you started running, as it is difficult to slow down and creates a potentially dangerous situation.

Attitude is important. A person's ability to do something difficult or strenuous is largely psychological. Always try to think positively because if you are convinced that you can do something, such as carrying a heavy load up a steep hill, you probably will succeed.

Because hiking and backpacking are strenuous activities which require quite a bit of energy, you should plan to replenish your energy as you use it. I usually carry a plastic bag of mixed dried fruits, candy and nuts (hikers call this Gorp), which I munch as I walk. You will probably enjoy experimenting with these ingredients to come up with a Gorp mixture that suits you.

You should make a short water and rest stop every hour or so, and more often in hot weather, to prevent dehydration and regain the used energy.

When hiking in cold weather, you will have to stop and peel off some clothes as soon as you get really warmed up so you won't sweat and get your underclothes wet. This is why you should dress in layers. Remove just the right amount of clothing to be comfortable. When you make a rest stop, you should immediately put plenty of clothing back on to prevent becoming chilled. When the weather is cold, be sure that you don't remove too much clothing because you will have to use more energy just to keep warm and may exhaust your energy supply. If this happens, you will not be able to keep warm when you stop, and hypothermia can set in quickly.

Be sure to drink plenty of water when hiking, in either hot or cold weather, to prevent dehydration. The higher the altitude, the more rapidly you lose water, and dehydration makes you more susceptible to altitude sickness and other altitude-related problems.

CAMPING MANNERS

A goal for all of us who use and enjoy our existing wilderness should be to keep it wild and unspoiled for future generations. We must minimize our impact, with the objective of leaving no signs of our visit. "Leave only footprints and take only pictures!" Those of us who go into the backcountry must help by taking the necessary precautions, setting good examples, and educating those who are ignorant of appropriate conduct.

Many of the following rules were taken from Sierra Club's "Camping Manners for Wilderness." These include conservation measures and camping conduct necessary for keeping our wild country clean and unscarred, and for making the trip enjoyable for all. There is a deep sense of satisfaction and personal achievement in the knowledge that you have camped in and traveled through an area without leaving visible traces of your passing.

Set up camp where foot traffic does the least damage to the fragile vegetation. Never camp in meadows; try to find a sandy or rocky area . Minimize building, whether for a kitchen or place to sleep. Don't modify the natural setting with rock walls for fireplaces or windbreaks. Don't cut limbs or small trees for tent poles or tarp supports; tie lines between two trees if you need a support, and don't put nails into trees. Don't disturb the soil with trenches, even though you may have been taught to always ditch your tent. Instead, locate your shelter or tent so water will drain away naturally. When you break camp, remove all evidence that you were there.

In many places you will find established campsites in the wilderness. Try to use one of these existing sites instead of making another.

Burying garbage is not acceptable. Park and Forest Services prohibit digging pits and burying trash. In many areas soil is too shallow; animals, wind and water expose the garbage, and distruping the soil may initiate erosion. Put food wrappers, foil, orange peels, etc. in your pocket, pack, ziplock bag or trash sack for later disposal. Where fires are permited, you can burn everything that will burn. Pack out everything that won't burn: cans, bottles, foil, egg shells, big pieces of plastic, etc. Foil does not burn, and some paper wrappers for food are laminated with foil. Attempts to burn foil produces so many little sparkling bits that it is impossible to pick all of them out of the ashes. Cans can be carried out more easily if they have been smashed flat with a rock, or both ends have been cut out and the can washed or burned and then flattened. Edibles may be scattered thinly, out of sight, and well away from camp and trail. Double check for litter-bits of paper, plastic, clothing, etc. Leave your campsite cleaner than it was when you found it. Make every trip a clean-up trip for campsite and trail.

GOVERNMENT AGENCIES

Apache-Sitgreaves National Forest
P.O. Box 640
Springerville, Arizona 85938

Bureau of Land Management
Safford Office
425 East 4th Street
Safford, Arizona 85546

Canyon de Chelly National Monument
Post Office Box 588
Chinle, Arizona 86503

Chiricahua National Monument
Dos Cabezas Star Route, Box 6500
Willcox, Arizona 85643

City of Phoenix
Outdoor Recreation Coordinator
2700 North 15th Avenue
Phoenix, Arizona 85007

Coconino National Forest
2323 Greenlaw Lane
Flagstaff, Arizona 86004

Coronado National Forest
300 W. Congress
Tucson, Arizona 85701

Coronado National Memorial
Route 2, Box 126
Hereford, Arizona 85615

Forth Bowie National Historical Site
Post Office Box 158
Bowie, Arizona 85605

Grand Canyon National Park
Post Office Box 129
Grand Canyon, Arizona 86023

Kaibab National Forest
800 South 6th Street
Williams, Arizona 86046

Kofa National Wildlife Refuge
Post Office Box 1032
Yuma, Arizona 85364

Navajo National Monument
Tonalea, Arizona 86044

Organ Pipe Cactus National Monument
Route 1, Box 100
Ajo, Arizona 85321

Petrified Forest National Park
Arizona 86028

Picacho Peak State Park
Post Office Box 275
Picacho, Arizona 85241

Prescott National Forest
344 South Cortez
Prescott, Arizona 86303

Rainbow Bridge National Monument
c/o Glen Canyon Natl. Recreation Area
Post Office Box 1507
Page, Arizona 86040

Saguaro National Monument
3693 S. Old Spanish Trail
Tucson, Arizona 85730

Tonto National Forest
2324 East McDowell
Post Office Box 5348
Phoenix, Arizona 85010

U.S. Geological Survey
Box 25286
Distribution Section
Denver Federal Center
Denver, Colorado 80225

Organ Pipe Cactus and rugged Sonoran Desert

Trail to Hidden Valley, South Mountain Park

Rugged country in the Chiricahuas

Weaver's Needle from Black Mesa Trail

— SQUAW PEAK SUMMIT

Round trip 2.4 miles
Part day, allow 3 hours
Approx. elevations 1,400–2,600
Season all year, but hot in summer

This small, rugged area is almost engulfed by Phoenix, but still makes a nice, close-in hike for the exercise and a sweeping view of the city.

From Lincoln Drive in Phoenix, turn onto Squaw Peak Drive. About 0.5 mile beyond the turnoff you should park on the left where the trailhead (Trail #300) is easily visible near the first ramada. The trail is also accessible at the Apache parking lot at the end of Squaw Peak Drive.

The trail starts switchbacking up through dry, rocky terrain and desert vegetation. In a few places the route goes through areas where the rock has tilted, fractured and then flaked off in geometric pieces. At about 0.5 mile, in a little saddle, the Squaw Peak Circumference Trail (Trail #302) intersects. This loop is 3.75 miles in length, climbs four passes, affords some spectacular scenery, and should be considered as a potential second trail to explore while in the area. To get to the summit, however, continue straight ahead.

As you climb the ridge, the view fans out over Phoenix and the close-by housing developments below. Shortly beyond the ridge the trail steepens. It climbs up the back side, comes to a little saddle and then swings back along the parking lot side of the hill.

Watch your footing near the top. The bare craggy rock provides an excellent viewpoint situated above the picnic area. As you face the picnic ramadas, South Mountain Park is ahead and to the right. The McDowell and Superstition Mountains are to your left, and the White Tanks are behind you to the right. Return by the same route.

In addition to the trails already mentioned, there is a self-guided nature trail (Trail #304) shown on the accompanying map. It features 20 numbered steel posts which describe various plants and animals common to this part of the desert. Guide books are available at the Squaw Peak Ranger Station.

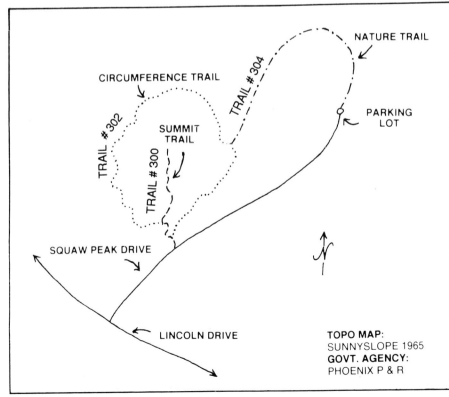

CIRCUMFERENCE TRAIL

NATURE TRAIL

TRAIL #304

TRAIL #302

SUMMIT TRAIL

TRAIL #300

PARKING LOT

SQUAW PEAK DRIVE

LINCOLN DRIVE

TOPO MAP:
SUNNYSLOPE 1965
GOVT. AGENCY:
PHOENIX P & R

2 — SOUTH MOUNTAIN PARK

Round trip 4 miles
Half day, allow 4 hours
Approx. elevations 2,200–2,000
Season all year, hot in summer

South Mountain Park consists of more than 17,000 acres of desert near metropolitan Phoenix. This hike passes through typical desert vegetation, involves a little rock-hopping down a desert wash and ends beyond an unusual tunnel. Keep in mind that the wash is a potential flood path, particularly during the summer monsoon season.

From the intersection of Baseline and Central avenues, head south on Central for about 2.3 miles to South Mountain Park and take Summit Road to the Buena Vista Lookout where there is a parking lot.

The hike begins at the Buena Vista Lookout, and the trail is part of the National Trail System (Trail #162). There is a sign in the parking area designating the trailhead at the start of the route to Hidden Valley. The terrain is dry and rocky, but the first part of the trail is well defined. On clear days, there are fine views of Phoenix from along here. The ratchety calls of cactus wrens and the trilling of canyon wrens are common trailside sounds, and vegetation in the area includes palo verdes, ocotillos, cholla and saguaro cacti. The first part of the hike is slightly downhill.

After about a mile, the trail drops down the righthand side of a pretty little canyon where catclaw acacia and canyon ragweed are common. There is a trail junction half a mile beyond where a sign indicates Hidden Valley-Fat Man Pass, but the route is not all that obvious. Drop over a large rock and into the bottom of the wash downstream. Continue to hike down the wash, and slide over some big, slick rocks into a sandy, sort of dish-shaped widening of the wash where there is desert vegetation and boulders. This is Hidden Valley.

The route continues down the valley which narrows until the wash exits through a tunnel formed by some huge boulders. The tunnel is about fifty feet long and a few feet wide—an interesting phenomenon that appeals to children and adults alike.

About fifty yards beyond the tunnel is a trail junction. This junction makes a good turn-around point.

Return by the same route.

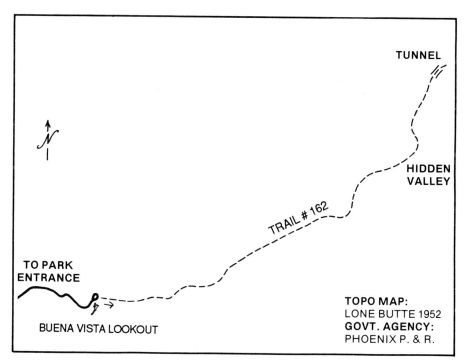

TUNNEL

HIDDEN VALLEY

TRAIL # 162

TO PARK
ENTRANCE

BUENA VISTA LOOKOUT

TOPO MAP:
LONE BUTTE 1952
GOVT. AGENCY:
PHOENIX P. & R.

3 — FOUR PEAKS

Round trip 6.6 miles
Half day, allow 6 hours
Elevations 5,700–7,000
Season May through October

A closely grouped formation of four peaks is visible in the far distance east of Phoenix. The drive to the trailhead plus the hike make a great all day trip.

From Mesa, drive north on State 87 (Beeline Highway) to where a large Forest Service sign between mileposts 202 and 203 indicates a desert vista. Depending on the season, the spring wildflower display may be beautiful in this area. Continue north on Highway 87 for 0.2 mile beyond the vista, and turn to the right onto F.S. #143. This is a rough road and four-wheel drive is strongly recommended. About 20 miles in on this road is a fork where a sign indicates one and one-fourth miles to Lone Pine Saddle. Turn right onto F.R. #648, and head south for about 1.3 miles to a parking area. The main Four Peaks Trail takes off to the left out of the parking lot and enters the newly created Four Peaks Wilderness. You, though, should take the newly constructed Browns Trail (Trail #133) which goes right from the parking area up the ridge.

The trail circles Knob 6988 and then drops to Browns Saddle. Views from along this section of the hike include Four Peaks, several lakes along the Salt River, Weaver's Needle in the Superstition Mountains, and the city of Phoenix.

The Amethyst Trail (Trail #253) diagonals in from the left, at Browns Saddle, and leads to an old amethyst mine. You, however, should continue straight ahead on the trail which angles down along the flanks of Four Peaks.

The next 1.4 miles tend to be downhill along the sides of the peaks. At about 3.3 miles there is a fence and a sign across the trail where it enters private property. Do not go beyond this point.

Return by the same route.

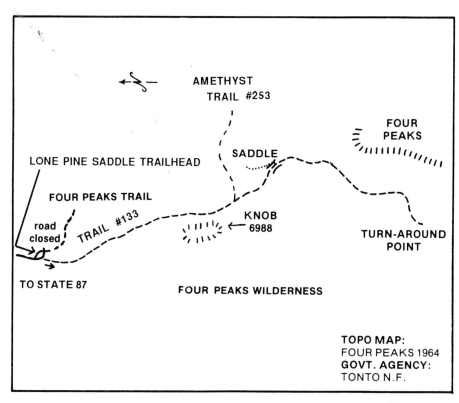

AMETHYST TRAIL #253

FOUR PEAKS

LONE PINE SADDLE TRAILHEAD

SADDLE

FOUR PEAKS TRAIL

road closed   TRAIL #133

KNOB 6988

TURN-AROUND POINT

TO STATE 87

FOUR PEAKS WILDERNESS

TOPO MAP:
FOUR PEAKS 1964
GOVT. AGENCY:
TONTO N.F.

4 — BLACK MESA

Round trip 5.2 miles
Half day, allow 5 hours
Elevations 2,200–2,740
Season all year, hot in summer

This is a very popular area and lends itself to many possible trips. Water is scarce, however, so be sure to take some with you. To get to the trailhead, go 5.4 miles northeast from Apache Junction, along Highway 88, to First Water Road (Forest Service Road #78). Turn right and proceed 2.6 miles to a barricade and parking area. The trail starts just past the gate, at road's end. First Water Road is a dirt thoroughfare and can be rough in places. Most vehicles, however, can make the trip if driven carefully.

Walk approximately 0.3 mile from the gate to a fork. The right hand fork is the Dutchman's Trail (Trail #104). You should bear left, however, onto the Second Water Trail (Trail #236).

Vegetation in the area includes saguaros, foothill palo verdes, barberry, buckhorn chollas and jojobas. There are several trails of use which enter and leave the first section of Second Water Trail, so be careful to stay on the main route. You will climb gradually to a little saddle at 0.7 mile, and the swing to the right, going diagonally downhill to a wash at 1.0 mile. The route heads north from the wash, up a small canyon, coming out in Garden Valley approximately 1.6 miles from the starting point. From there the journey traverses the relatively level floor of Garden Valley to a junction at 1.8 miles. The intersection should be fairly obvious. Second Water Trail continues north from here, but you should turn right onto the Black Mesa Trail (Trail #241).

Black Mesa Trail climbs gradually in a southeasterly direction toward the edge of Black Mesa, then steadily upward along its side, above Garden Valley. Saguaros and teddy bear cholla are abundant and there are outstanding views back toward Garden Valley and off to the right.

The trail levels out at 2.9 miles and this makes a good place to turn around. Black Mesa Trail eventually intersects the Dutchman's Trail, near Palomino Mountain, but you should not attempt that trek unless you have additional information. There is a dense forest of cholla in this area, and Weaver's Needle roars up on the distance ahead—one of the finest views you will have of it.

Return by the same route.

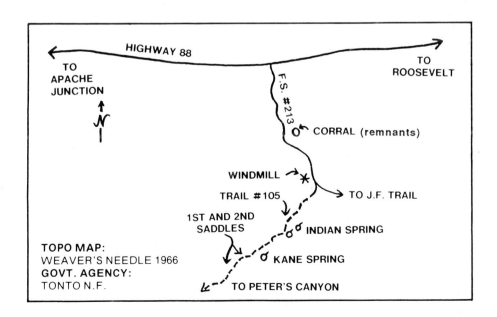

5 — TORTILLA RANCH

Round trip 4.4 miles
Half day, allow 5 hours
Approx. elevations 3,100–3,800
Season all year, hot in summer

This is one of the more peaceful hikes in the Superstition Mountains. It is less accessible and, therefore, not so frequented by the treasure hunting set. The hike described here will serve as a good introduction to the area.

To get to the trailhead from Apache Junction, take Highway 88 (The Apache Trail) for about 23 miles to a dirt road taking off on the right between mileposts 221 and 222. This is Tortilla Road (F.S. Road #213). Four-wheel drive will be necessary from here to the trailhead, since it is very rough. Proceed about 2.3 miles to the Old Tortilla Headquarters, where the remnants of an old corral complex will be seen.

From there continue on the main road which swings somewhat to the left another 0.5 mile. At that point, turn right and go 0.1 mile to the windmill at Tortilla Well. Park there and begin hiking on Peter's Trail (Trail #105), which starts across the fence on the other side of the windmill.

The first part of the trail is gradually uphill, hemmed in by hillsides on either side. It soon follows a wash, however,

crossing it several times. Sycamores and an occasional Fremont cottonwood grow along the wash, and seepwillows can also be seen where there are reliable pools of water.

There is a fork in the drainage at 0.6 mile, and the route may be vague for a short stretch. Simply follow the right fork and you will soon be able to see where the trail exits on the south side. From there it pulls away from the wash to drier, more open terrain. The hike gradually progresses uphill, following a drainage and passing Kane Spring where there are a few cottonwoods for shade. There are also several nice thickets of sugar sumac near the spring.

The grade becomes increasingly steep until, just before the 2 mile point, the climb tapers off somewhat. The route reaches a saddle at 2.1 miles, then drops down a short distance before climbing to another small saddle at 2.2 miles. This is a good turn around point. Peter's Trail continues from here, eventually climbing Peter's Divide, passing through a section at Peter's Canyon, and finally ending at a junction with the Dutchman's Trail, deep in the heart of the western Superstitions. Don't tackle this much longer hike unless you have obtained additional information and are well prepared.

Return by the same route.

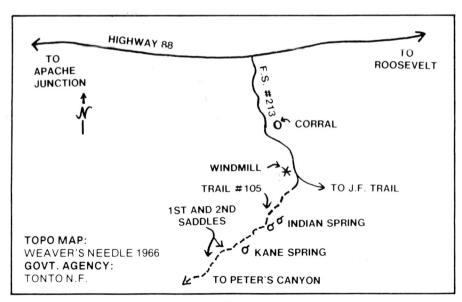

24

6 — WEAVER'S NEEDLE

Round Trip 4.6 miles
Part day, allow 4 hours
Approx elevations 2,400-3,800
Season all year, hot in summer

Playing an important part in the many legends of the Superstition Mountains is Weaver's Needle, a huge volcanic plug nestled deep within the center of this most rugged mountain range. One of the best known such stories is that of Jacob Waltz, a nineteenth century prospector who supposedly found a fortune in gold somewhere in the Superstitions. Over the years, Waltz made a number of productive trips to his mine and eventually sealed it, never to return. Since then, whether or not the mine actually existed, these mountains have been picked, shoveled, blasted and scraped by thousands of treasure seekers hoping to locate it.

One of the best views of Weaver's Needle is from Fremont Saddle, on the Peralta Trail. To get there, take Highway 60-89 east from the town of Apache Junction about 8.3 miles to Peralta Road (Forest Service Road #77). Proceed northeast on Peralta Road 5.5 miles to a fork, where you should bear left, remaining on F.S. #77. Continue another 1.9 miles to the parking area at the end of the road, just past Don's Camp.

The Peralta Trail (Trail #102) begins at the upper end of the parking area, and gradually climbs through a saguaro-palo verde community, crossing and re-crossing the wash in the bottom of the canyon. Keep in mind that this canyon could be a dangerous floodpath in stormy weather. There are thickets of sugar sumac along the wash, and the canyon bottom is a jumble of huge, thought-provoking boulders that have tumbled from the cliffs above. The trail continues to climb.

At about 1.8 miles the route pulls away from the canyon floor and switchbacks up to Fremont Saddle, at 2.3 miles. The trail occasionally cuts across solid rock which sometimes makes footing a little unstable, so be careful. Weaver's Needle is obscured until almost the last minute. At the saddle, however, there is an unobstructed view of it, and, after having seen it from this perspective, there will be little doubt as to why it has played such an important part in so many of the Superstition Mountains legends.

The Peralta Trail continues into Boulder Canyon and eventually intersects the Dutchman's Trail, many miles away. Fremont Saddle, however, makes a good turn around point for the day hiker. Return by the same route.

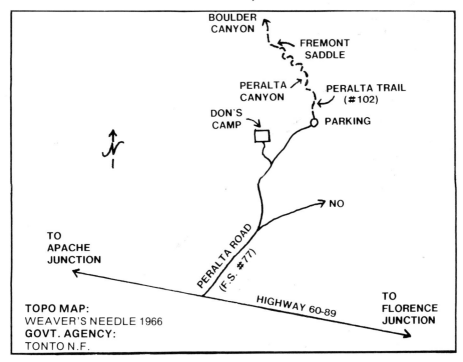

BOULDER CANYON

FREMONT SADDLE

PERALTA CANYON

PERALTA TRAIL (#102)

DON'S CAMP

PARKING

NO

TO APACHE JUNCTION

PERALTA ROAD (F.S. #77)

HIGHWAY 60-89

TO FLORENCE JUNCTION

TOPO MAP:
WEAVER'S NEEDLE 1966
GOVT. AGENCY:
TONTO N.F.

25

7 — BULL PASTURE

Round trip 4.1 miles
Part day, allow 3 hours
Approx. elevations 2,400–3,100
Season all year but hot in summer

Bull Pasture is situated in the Ajo Mountains, a rugged volcanic range along the eastern boundary of Organ Pipe Cactus National Monument. The present route was constructed in 1953. However, cattlemen used the area known as Bull Pasture for years until it was abandoned in the 1920s.

Follow the Ajo Mountain Drive from U.S. 85 in the National Monument to the trailhead. This is a 10.7 mile drive through Sonoran Desert country. Vegetation consists mainly of thorny plants adapted to a land of much sun and little water—mesquites, catclaws, palo verdes, ocotillos, saguaros, Engelmann's prickly pear, Coville's barrel cacti and the organ pipe cacti for which the monument is named. There is a bustling bird life in the early mornings, and the spring wildflower display may be lavish in some years.

The trail takes off from the road and soon comes to a fork. Take the righthand fork. The route climbs most of the way, quite steeply at times. There is wildlife to be seen along the trail if you hike slowly and take time to observe. On one hike here we saw a coyote, velvet ants, a walking stick, numerous grasshoppers, a red-spotted toad and many birds, including Gambel's quail, rock wrens, a kestrel, a red-tailed hawk and a brown towhee.

Near the one mile point you will reach a pass where the Estes Canyon Trail drops down on the left. Continue ahead on the main trail which soon begins switchbacking up to Bull Pasture.

From the sloping shelf of Bull Pasture, there are good views of the Ajo Mountains. The high point in the range is Mount Ajo, elevation 4,808 feet. Desert bighorn sheep may occasionally be seen moving nimbly about on the high, sheer cliffs.

Return via the switchbacks to the Estes Canyon juntion and take the Estes Canyon Trail to the right. It switchbacks steeply to the canyon bottom, then proceeds gradually downhill. The trail becomes a thready route through the chain-fruit cholla along the wash. The route tends to the left, eventually rejoining the Bull Pasture Trail at the fork. Retrace your steps from here to the parking area just beyond.

From the parking area, Ajo Mountain Drive continues its loop for approximately 9 miles back to U.S. 85.

ESTES CANYON

BULL PASTURE

TOPO MAP:
MOUNT AJO 1963
GOVT. AGENCY:
NATIONAL PARK SERVICE

TO 85

8 — SIX-SHOOTER CANYON

Round Trip 9.4 miles
All Day or backpack, allow 8-9 hours
Approx. elevations 4,800-7,600
Season April through November

This is a challenging hike, climbing almost 3,000 feet in 4.7 miles. The beautiful scenery and outstanding views, however, help make up for the difficulty. The trail goes through a number of vegetation life zones, with scrub brush and oak in the lower elevations and juniper, pine, fir and aspen higher up. During the summer, days can be extremely hot, while, in the winter, it is usually cold, with a possibility of snow. For those reasons, spring and fall are generally regarded as the best times for this hike.

To get to the trailhead, take Jess Hayes Road southeast from Globe to where F.S. Road #112 intersects F.S. Road #222, about 2.5 miles from town. From there, bear right, on Road #112 (Icehouse Canyon Road) and proceed 6.3 miles. Road #55 will intersect at the 2.4 mile mark, and the Icehouse Canyon Picnic Area will be encountered just past 5 miles. Immediately before reaching a little bridge, at the given mileage, there is a place to park on the left. The trailhead is about ten yards past the bridge, on the right, and is Forest Service Trail #197.

The journey starts in a southwest direction and parallels a creek for quite a distance. It isn't long before you encounter a series of switchbacks, and, as you proceed, it will be necessary to cross the creek a number of times. Water runs through here and there are usually a number of little waterfalls along the way.

After having hiked 0.8 mile, the trail forks. Take the right branch and follow it up and around the steep ridge. This part of the trek will afford you with many spectacular views of Globe, Miami and Claypool, as well as the surrounding countryside. Approximately 1 mile farther along, the route crosses through a saddle and proceeds around another ridge. Along here, there are more outstanding viewpoints.

Just before reaching the 3 mile point, the trail meets a fence and parallels it for a distance. Another one-half mile along the way, you will find yourself on an old abandoned logging road, in a thickly wooded area. A flooded mine shaft will be seen at the 3.7 mile mark, and 0.1 mile past the mine, on the right, Telephone Trail (#192) intersects. This is the route to Icehouse Canyon, but you should bear left, staying on the four-wheel drive road.

The trail ends at Ferndell Spring, just a short distance north of the Upper Pinal Campground. It is a small campground, providing only six sites, but offers tables, restrooms and water, from May through October. It is a great place to spend some time.

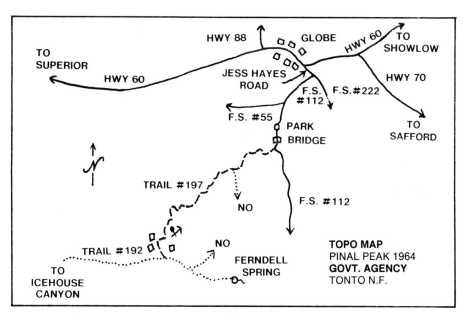

9 — PALM CANYON

Round trip 1.5 miles
Part day, allow 2 hours
Approx. elevations 2,100–2,500
Season all year, hot in summer

A relatively short hike into a rugged canyon in the Kofa Mountains will provide a glimpse of Arizona's largest stands of native California fan palms. There are other stands of these palms in a few isolated places in California, but there are only two places in Arizona where such native fan palms occur. This is one of them.

Head south on State 95 from I-10 in the town of Quartzsite. Before leaving Quartzsite, you may want to stop at an interesting memorial to "Hi Jolly," a famous camel driver. Proceed south on 95 for about 19 miles to a dirt road which goes left (east) to Palm Canyon. (This same junction can be reached by driving north on 95 for about 60 miles from I-8 in Yuma.) Continue for about 9 miles to a parking area at the end of the road.

The trail takes off from the end of the road, heading uphill and more or less following the righthand side of the wash. Vegetation in the area includes saguaros, ocotillos, brittlebush, various chollas, palo verdes, ironwoods, jojobas, yuccas, catclaws, Mormon tea and beavertail prickly pear. The ground is rocky, and the trail may be faint in places as it climbs the canyon, hemmed in on either side by immense rock walls.

About 0.5 mile from the trailhead is a nice stand of palms in a cleft on the left side of the canyon. A little scrambling up the main canyon will disclose palms in clefts on both sides. These palms have developed long root systems to keep from being washed away during summer storms and to tap water during long periods of drought.

If you wish to explore further, you should be extremely cautious as there are many cliffs where the trees are growing. Return is by the same route. Additional hikes in the Kofas should be made in the company of an experienced guide because the range is deceivingly steep and rugged.

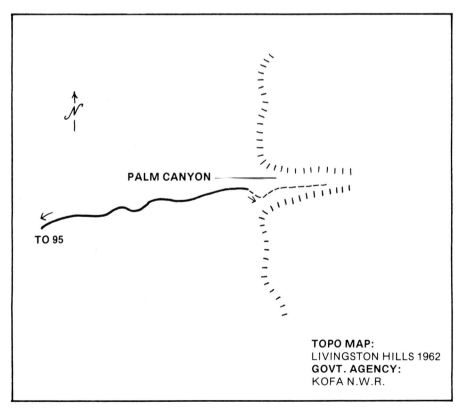

PALM CANYON

TO 95

TOPO MAP:
LIVINGSTON HILLS 1962
GOVT. AGENCY:
KOFA N.W.R.

10 — PICACHO PEAK

Round trip 4 miles
Half day, allow 6 hours
Approx. elevations 2,000–3,400
Season all year, hot in summer

The only Civil War battle to take place in Arizona was fought at the base of Picacho Peak, a prominent landmark off I-10, northwest of Tucson. Hikers should have good boots or hiking shoes and water before tackling this steep route over precarious footing. In only two miles you climb 1800 feet. It is also advisable that you check with the park ranger before starting the hike.

Take Picacho Peak Road from I-10 and take exit 219. Follow the signs to the park where there is an entrance fee of three dollar charge per vehicle. To get to the trailhead, continue past the park office to a road fork. Turn left here onto Barrett Scenic Loop and continue 0.4 mile from the fork to a parking area.

The Hunter Trail to Picacho Peak heads up to the left of a water tank. Vegetation is typical of the Sonoran Desert and includes teddy bear chollas, jumping chollas, creasote bushes, ocotillos, saugaros, and foothill palo verdes. Follow the steep, twisting route uphill.

At 0.5 mile the trail reaches the base of some light-colored cliffs. It then swings to the left along the base of some cliffs higher up. From there it goes to the right to a saddle at 0.9 mile.

The route drops down the other side from the saddle and is marked by arrows. Parts of the trail is very steep and indefinite. Loose rock may make the footing slippery. Proceed down along the base of the cliff, then left around to a trail junction where another trail comes up from the road below. The main trail proceeds uphill.

Several sets of double steel cables anchored into the rock provide hand holds where the route climbs bare rock. After the last cable climb, the trail continues up to the top of the peak. The summit is bare except for a few thorny bushes along the verges, and it is a sheer drop from the summit to the desert floor where traffic roars along the interstate. Having perched atop Picacho and felt its isolation and detachment from the life whizing past its base, we mentally re-climb it and enjoy it again whenever we drive past.

Return by the same route.

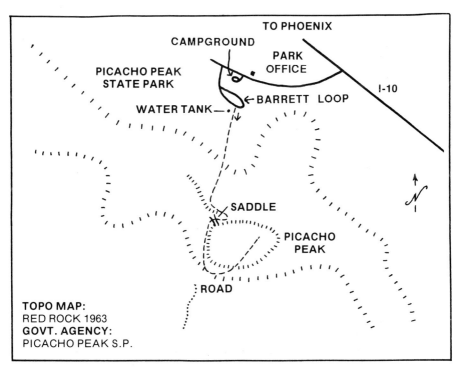

TOPO MAP:
RED ROCK 1963
GOVT. AGENCY:
PICACHO PEAK S.P.

11 — BUTTERFLY TRAIL

Round trip 11.4 miles
All day, allow 8 hours
Approx. elevations 6,500-8,200
Season May through October

This is a pretty hike, passing through forests of ponderosa pine and Douglas fir, woodlands of oak and juniper. It is a pleasant mixture of sunshine and shade, open and sheltered, moist and dry. Of course, there are wildflowers and butterflies in varying numbers depending on the time of year.

Take Tanque Verde Road from Tucson and turn onto the Catalina Highway. Proceed to the base of the Catalina Mountains where the route becomes Mount Lemmon Highway at milepost 0. Continue about 20 miles to Palisades Ranger Station. The trailhead is on the righthand side of the highway next to a parking area.

A well-defined trail climbs for half a mile through a ponderosa pine forest to a saddle. There is a fork at the saddle where a short trail goes to the lookout on Mount Bigelow on the left; but take the trail which diagonals to the right, destined for Soldier Camp.

It drops down to the cooler side of the mountain which is forested with Douglas fir. Columbines and violets grow in the shaded areas, and raspberries grow in some of the sunny clearings. The trail leaves the fir forest now and then where the terrain is dry and exposed. Netleaf oaks, nolinas and grasses are more common in these areas.

The general trend is downhill. At 2.5 miles is a junction where Potato Patch Trail goes to the right; bear left here. Arizona madrones, alligator junipers, yuccas and oaks grow on ridges along here. As the trail continues, there are several small canyons along its lower reaches where inland boxelders, Arizona walnuts and bigtooth maples grow. There may be some running water here.

Soon the trail begins the climb to Soldier Camp and becomes rather steep in places. Crystal Spring Trail goes to the right about 1.4 miles from Soldier Camp, but stay on the Butterfly.

At trail's end is a dirt road which goes out to the Mount Lemmon Highway a quarter mile distant.

Return by the same route unless transportation has been arranged beforehand.

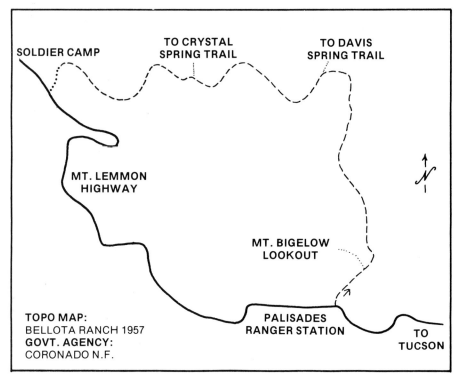

SOLDIER CAMP

TO CRYSTAL
SPRING TRAIL

TO DAVIS
SPRING TRAIL

MT. LEMMON
HIGHWAY

MT. BIGELOW
LOOKOUT

N

TOPO MAP:
BELLOTA RANCH 1957
GOVT. AGENCY:
CORONADO N.F.

PALISADES
RANGER STATION

TO
TUCSON

12 — GREEN MOUNTAIN

Round trip 8 miles
All day, allow 6 hours
Approx. elevations 6,000-7,300
Season May through October

The rugged east side of the Catalina Mountains gets less traffic than the canyons lower down and the developed areas farther up.

Take Tanque Verde Road from Tucson and turn onto the Catalina Highway. Proceed to the base of the Catalina Mountains where the route becomes the Mount Lemmon Highway at milepost 0. Continue about 12 miles and turn into General Hitchcock Picnic Area which is on the right between highway mileposts 12 and 13. There is a parking area at the road's end, and the trail takes off through the picnic ground toward a green water tank. Go about 30 feet beyond the tank, then cross the creek to the right.

The route goes gradually upstream through a forest of oaks, firs, Arizona walnuts and ponderosa pines. About half a mile upstream, the trail pulls away from the left side of the canyon bottom and climbs through drier country where nolina and manzanita are common. The manzanita is easily identified by its rich red branches. The name is Spanish meaning "little apples," which refers to the plant's small, round fruits.

It is uphill to Bear Saddle at the 2-mile point. Head left at the saddle. About a quarter mile beyond is a faint trail going off to Maverick Spring on the right, but continue left on the main trail.

Another 0.4 mile down the hillside is another trail junction where a poor trail goes to the right toward Brush Corral. Continue on the main trail for about 1.2 miles to another junction where another trail goes to the right toward Brush Corral. The Green Mountain Trail switchbacks uphill through netleaf oaks, silverleaf oaks, ponderosa pines and Douglas firs. About 500 feet above the Brush Corral junction, the trail passes the closed-off fork that was the **old** Green Mountain Trail. Continue on the main trail as it climbs for 0.3 mile beyond the Brush Corral junction, then drops down for a little over 200 feet to San Pedro Vista. From the last stretch of trail there are some good views of the San Pedro Valley off to the right and the Galiuro Mountains beyond. There are a number of tall, picturesque rock formations towering above the trees in this area.

Return by the same route unless transportation arrangements have been made beforehand.

TO PALISADES RANGER STATION

SAN PEDRO VISTA

TO BRUSH CORRAL

TO MAVERICK SPRING

BEAR SADDLE

MT. LEMMON HIGHWAY

N

TOPO MAP:
BELLOTA RANCH 1957
GOVT. AGENCY:
CORONADO N.F.

TO TUCSON

13 — ASPEN LOOP

Round trip 3.6 miles
Half day, allow 4 hours
Approx. elevations 7,400-8,200
Season April through November

This hike climbs through a beautiful aspen grove and returns along a creek bordered by maples and alders. It makes a nice afternoon outing, particularly in the fall when the aspens and maples are turning.

Take Tanque Verde Road from Tucson and turn onto the Catalina Highway. Proceed to the base of the Catalina Mountains where the route becomes the Mount Lemmon Highway at milepost 0. Continue up the Mount Lemmon Highway to Summerhaven, keeping left at the Summerhaven-Ski Valley junction. Drive down the road through Summerhaven to Marshall Gulch Picnic Area. **NOTE:** The picnic area may be closed due to pollution problems. If this is the case, the road will be closed off, making it necessary to hike about 0.5 mile down the road to the trailhead.

Aspen Trail begins next to the restroom on the righthand side of the parking area at Marshall Gulch. It climbs diagonally uphill for a little less than 100 yards to a fork of sorts. Keep to the right (uphill) at this "fork." The area is forested with Douglas fir, Gambel's oak and limber pine. Silverleaf oak grows on the drier hillsides.

At 0.4 mile the trail passes through a grove of large aspens and switchbacks uphill into ponderosa pines and oaks. It continues to climb, then becomes more level or downhill as it nears a junction of sorts at 1.5 miles. Here a faint trail diagonals off to the left to Lunch Ledge; Aspen Trail continues on the right to Marshall Saddle at 2.4 miles.

Several trails intersect at the saddle which is in an open, sunny forest of ponderosa pines. Take the righthand fork which drops steadily downhill and soon parallels a small creek. The area of the creek is thicketed with Arizona alders, bigtooth maples and willows. There are tall spars of white fir and open, grassy areas that may be strewn with wildflowers. Water striders ply the surfaces of the pools, their bodies often casting rather large shadows on the bottom. These insects have small hairs on their legs which do not break the water's surface.

At 3.6 miles the trail comes back into Marshall Gulch Picnic Area near where the hike began.

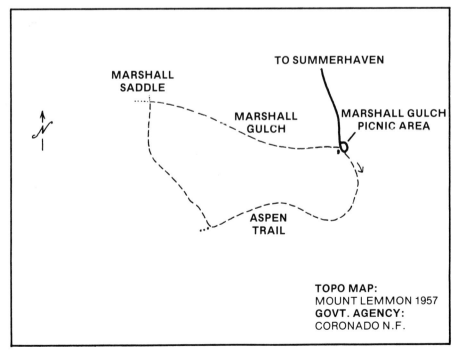

TO SUMMERHAVEN

MARSHALL
SADDLE

MARSHALL
GULCH

MARSHALL GULCH
PICNIC AREA

ASPEN
TRAIL

TOPO MAP:
MOUNT LEMMON 1957
GOVT. AGENCY:
CORONADO N.F.

14 — SHOVEL SPRING

Round trip 6.6 miles
Half day or backpack, allow 5 hours
Approx. elevations 9,100-7,500
Season May through October

The destination of this hike is a spring near a small cabin built by the Arizona Game and Fish Department. The spring provides water for wildlife and is tucked back in a small, forested canyon.

From Tucson, take Tanque Verde Road to the Catalina Highway. Proceed on Catalina Highway to the base of the Catalina Mountains where it becomes the Mount Lemmon Highway at milepost 0. Continue about 25 miles to the Ski Valley-Summerhaven junction and turn right toward Ski Valley. About 3 miles farther, there is a parking area on the left about 0.1 mile before the entrance to the Mount Lemmon Observatory. **NOTE:** There is another parking area on the left a short distance before the correct one. The entrance to the observatory is visible from the parking area.

Near the parking area is a gate. Walk around it and follow the two-track road on the right which parallels the chain-link fence along the perimeter of the observatory. At the end of this stretch of fence is a woodland trail taking off to the left.

This is a cool, moist area forested by white and Douglas firs. The numerous mounds of earth are the work of valley pocket gophers. When you have come 0.6 mile from the fence, the trail joins another two-track road. Turn to the right and continue for about three quarters of a mile to a trail junction. Take the wide righthand fork which, after a short distance, begins a series of rapidly descending switchbacks for a quarter mile. There is a little "saddle" here where the road heads uphill on the other side. Continue on the road for about 100 feet beyond the middle of the saddle, then the trail diagonals off to the left.

At the next two junctions, take the righthand forks and continue along the trail which meanders through open pine forest down to Shovel Spring. The spring is located just up the canyon from the cabin.

Return by the same route.

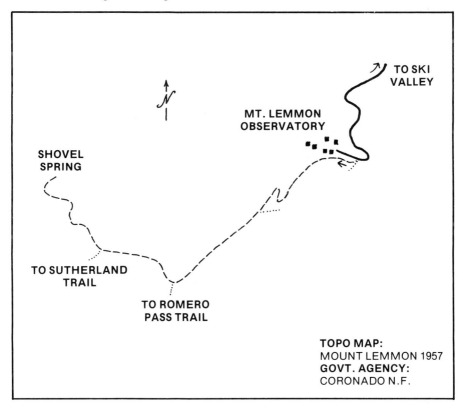

TOPO MAP:
MOUNT LEMMON 1957
GOVT. AGENCY:
CORONADO N.F.

15 — SEVEN FALLS

Round trip 8.2 miles
Half day, allow 6 hours
Approx. elevations 2,700–3,360
Season all year, hot in summer

Seven water falls, interspersed by pools, are created by the creek in Bear Canyon as it cascades over a series of rocks in a steep desert drainage. Situated in the lower reaches of the Catalina Mountains north of Tucson, the area is popular and may be crowded, especially on weekends. Many generations of Tucsonians have hiked into the falls to picnic and swim, though it is not advisable to swim or dive here because of the unstable footing, concealed rocks and debris carried down by flood waters.

To get to the trailhead from the junction of Tanque Verde Road and Sabino Canyon Road in Tucson, proceed about 5 miles on Sabino Canyon Road to the Sabino Canyon Visitor Center parking lot. The trail commences on the east end of the lot, past the dumpsters, and parallels the now closed road to Lower Bear Picnic Area. The trail abuts the boundary fence until you get to the Bear Canyon Loop, about 1.7 miles. If you do not wish to hike the 3.4 mile round trip distance from the visitor center to the Lower Bear Picnic Area, the Forest Service provides an hourly shuttle bus along the route, between 9 a.m. and 4 p.m., for a small fee.

From Lower Bear, there is a sign designating the trail, and it is clearly defined as it starts up the canyon in the vicinity of the creek. The creek is often dry, or there may be a few small pools of water dammed among the rocks. Keep in mind that this canyon is a potentially dangerous flood path during the summer monsoon season. Desert vegetation is lush—foothill palo verde, brittlebush, saguaro, honey mesquite, Englemann prickly pear, catclaw acacia, ocotillo, canyon ragweed, heartleaf jatropha and several species of cholla. In the immediate area of the creek are sycamores, willows and a few Fremont cottonwoods.

The trail more or less parallels the creek, crossing back and forth a number of times via random stepping stones. The grade is gradually uphill, and heavy rounded boulders in the drainage are evidence of the creek's potentially mean disposition. There are rugged cliffs on all sides where saguaros and teddy bear chollas are common.

At 3.3 miles, the trail switchbacks up a hillside, then continues to parallel the creek from higher up. Looking back down the canyon, the city of Tucson can be seen sprawling out from the foothills and parts of the Tucson Mountains and Baboquivari Peak are visible in the distance.

At 3.9 miles, there is a trail fork where the upper route continues for about 5 miles to Sycamore Dam. The left fork drops down and ends at the base of Seven Falls, 4.1 miles from the visitor center. There is a large pool here, at the foot of the falls, skimmed by dragonflies and bordered by scattered willow. Lizards and other sunbathers lounge on the big, light-colored rocks on warm days.

Return by the same route.

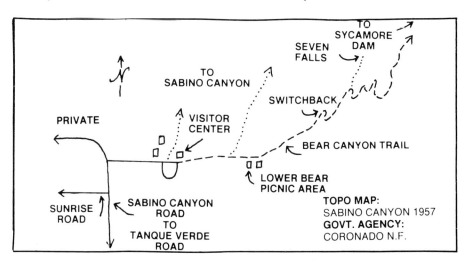

16 — PIMA CANYON

Round trip 6.1 miles
Half day, allow 5 hours
Approx. elevations 2,900-4,000
Season all year, hot in summer

This rugged desert canyon is a very popular area near Tucson. As the canyon rises through the Catalina foothills, it affords a close-in opportunity to view the city from above while hiking through an interesting desert environment.

From the intersection of Ina and Oracle roads in Tucson, drive north on Oracle Road for about 1 mile and turn right onto Magee Road. The cleft visible in the mountains ahead is Pima Canyon. Proceed 1.6 miles to a parking area at the end of Magee Road.

Hike beyond the parking area on the blocked-off dirt road for about 130 yards to where this road is intersected by another coming down the hill. A trail starts just beyond this intersecting road. Continue on the trail for 0.2 mile from the road to a barbed-wire fence and the National Forest boundary. The trail climbs gradually for about half a mile, affording fine views of Tucson to the south. At about 1 mile, the path rounds a rocky area and drops into the bottom of Pima Canyon where there may be a trickle of water.

The route meanders back and forth across the wash, ascending gradually. There will be some route-finding involved, but the trail is seldom far from the bottom of the wash. (These desert washes are unsafe if rain is likely, particularly during the monsoon season.)

Desert plant and animal life is prolific in this area. Harris ground squirrels are common, and many large and unusual insects lumber about their business among the saguaros and palo verdes. The canyon attracts an unusual variety of birds, making this an especially good hike for carrying binoculars and field guides.

At about 3 miles is the first large Mexican blue oak. Not far beyond is a small catchment dam. The trail continues up the canyon from here, but much route-finding is necessary, and this spot makes a good turn-around point.

Return by the same route.

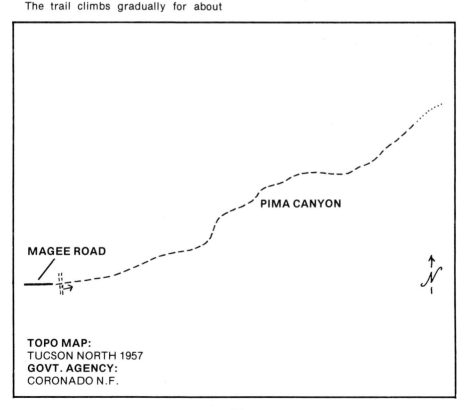

MAGEE ROAD

PIMA CANYON

TOPO MAP:
TUCSON NORTH 1957
GOVT. AGENCY:
CORONADO N.F.

17 — DOUGLAS SPRING TRAIL

Round trip 15 miles
All day, allow 9 hours
Approx. elevations 2,700–6,200
Season all year, hot in summer

On July 5, 1989, a lightning strike ignited a fire which consumed 7,500 acres within Saguaro National Monument. The Douglas Spring Trail and Campground were in the area that was burned. The trail and campground were recently reopened, but travel is now restricted to the trail, in order to allow complete revegetation and prevent rogue trails. This hike now offers an excellent opportunity to view the effects of wildfire in the Desert Scrub, Desert Grassland, Oak Woodland and Pine-Oak Woodland. A permit must be obtained from the visitor center at Saguaro National Monument if you plan an overnight stay.

From Speedway and Wilmot in Tucson, proceed east on Speedway for about 9.7 miles to a parking area on the right. The public road ends here before the turn-off to a private guest ranch. An interpretive sign marks the trailhead.

The route starts out across a desert area where you will spot several species of cacti, as well as desert birds and other wildlife. Due to the fire, the wildlife and vegetation are not as abundant as before, but occasional crew-cactus wrens, curve-billed thrashers, and Gambel's quail can be seen, as can flocks of purple martins feeding on flying insects.

After about three quarters of a mile, the trail steepens a little. Near here, the route heads up what is obviously an old road. About 200 yards up the road, keep an eye out for the point where the trail takes off on the left.

The climb is not too steep as it continues to Douglas Spring, elevation 4,800 feet. The water is seasonal, but this grassy area studded with big rocks makes a pleasant rest stop and camping area.

Shortly beyond the camping area, the trail becomes steeper and climbs steadily to Cowhead Saddle. Manzanitas, junipers and pinyons were once common on these hillsides, and Arizona madrones, Chihuahua pines and silverleaf oaks once stood where the saddle is approached via a series of switchbacks. There are no views from Cowhead Saddle, but it provides a good spot on the flanks of the Rincons to end the hike. A trail heads left to Manning Camp from here. Another goes right and down Tanque Verde Ridge, but this makes a good turn-around point for the dayhiker.

Return by the same route.

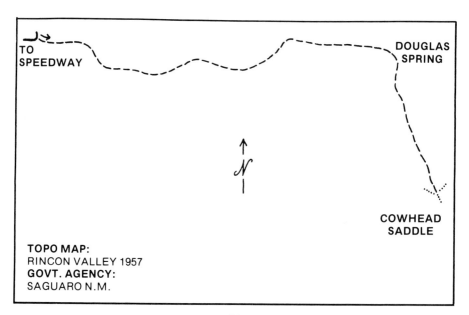

TO SPEEDWAY

DOUGLAS SPRING

COWHEAD SADDLE

TOPO MAP:
RINCON VALLEY 1957
GOVT. AGENCY:
SAGUARO N.M.

18 — JUNIPER BASIN

Round trip 13 miles
All day, allow 8 hours
Approx. elevations 3,600–6,000
Season all year

This hike is in the Rincon Mountains, within easy distance of Tucson. It starts in the desert foothills and climbs Tanque Verde Ridge into juniper and pinyons at Juniper Basin. An entrance fee for access to the Tanque Verde Ridge Trail is collected just beyond the Rincon Mountain visitor center, and, in addition, a permit must be obtained at the visitor center if you plan an overnight stay.

Take Old Spanish Trail from Tucson and follow the signs to Saguaro National Monument. Just beyond the entrance station the road forks. Straight ahead is the one-way, eight mile Cactus Forest Loop Drive. You should bear right 1.8 miles to the Javelina Picnic Area and the Tanque Verde Ridge Trailhead.

The trail takes off on the righthand side of the road and climbs among palo verdes, ocotillos, jojobas, and catclaws. Cacti are especially common along this trail—saguaros, prickly pears, fishhook barrels, and staghorn cholla among others. In late spring, the lavender blooms of the Fendler's hedgehogs make their flowering

neighbors seem pale by comparison.

The route climbs steadily, providing broadening views of Tucson. Occasionally, a collard lizard may be seen sunning on a rock.

At about 2.5 miles, the desert vegetation has yielded to grassland species such as nolina, sotol, and shin dagger. In the next mile, a few junipers and rosewood trees have come into the landscape.

Shortly beyond the 5,000-foot elevation, the trail passes through a little basin where the vegetation changes again and is comprised of manzanita, silk tassel, Emory oak, Mexican pinyon pine, juniper and shrub live oak. We also noticed some cream pincushion cacti—an inobvious species unless you're looking for it. It is round and rather flat, barely protruding above the ground.

By now the steeper sections of the trail are interspersed by relatively level areas. Juniper Basin is a level area at the 6.5-mile point, appropriately named for the weathered old alligator junipers in the area.

The trail continues to Cowhead Saddle and Manning Camp, but Juniper Basin makes a good turn-around point for the dayhiker.

Return by the same route.

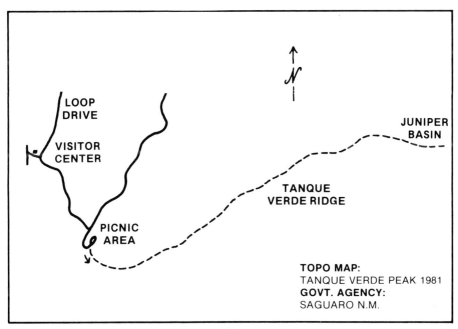

LOOP DRIVE

VISITOR CENTER

JUNIPER BASIN

TANQUE VERDE RIDGE

PICNIC AREA

TOPO MAP:
TANQUE VERDE PEAK 1981
GOVT. AGENCY:
SAGUARO N.M.

19 — WASSON PEAK

Round trip 9.6 miles
All day, allow 5 hours
Approx. elevations 2,600-4,700
Season all year, hot in summer

Wasson Peak is the high point in the Tucson Mountains. Part of this low desert range is located in the western section of Saguaro National Monument. Its closeness to Tucson makes this a convenient Saturday or Sunday hike.

From I-10 in Tucson, head west on Speedway through Gates Pass. Turn right at a well-marked intersection about 9 miles from I-10 and follow signs to Saguaro National Monument. Continue past the information center to where a sign indicates the Bajada Loop. Turn to the right and proceed 0.8 mile to parking on the right.

The trail takes off from the parking area. Vegetation at the start is typical of the saguaro-palo verde community. Gila woodpeckers, cactus wrens, canyon wrens, curve-billed thrashers, coyotes, javelina and deer are all residents of the area.

Ascending a series of steep switchbacks soon affords a fine view of Avra Valley in the distance. At 1.5 miles the grade tapers off. In another mile, Wasson Peak comes into view. At 2.7 miles, continue straight where three different trails intersect. Picacho Peak is visible in the far distance. Grasses, sotol, ocotillo, shin dagger and catclaw are common along here. White-throated swifts nest in cliffs between here and the summit of Wasson. Keep an eye out for these streamlined brown and white birds that rocket over the ridges.

There are some old mine tailings below the trail just before it begins a series of switchbacks. Stay clear of the area; the old workings are unstable.

Just after reaching the top of the switchbacks, a panoramic view of Tucson opens up--the view that makes this a popular hike. Turn left and proceed 0.3 mile to the 4,687-foot summit of Wasson Peak. Both Baboquivari and Kitt peaks can be seen from here.

Return by the same route.

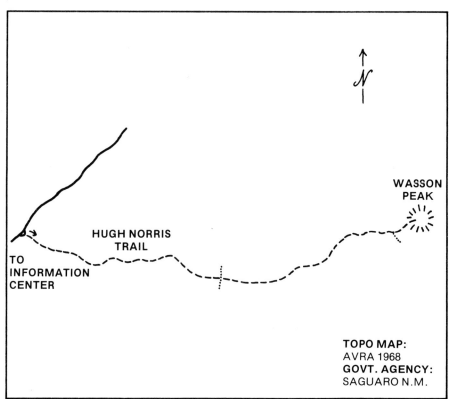

N

WASSON PEAK

HUGH NORRIS TRAIL

TO INFORMATION CENTER

TOPO MAP:
AVRA 1968
GOVT. AGENCY:
SAGUARO N.M.

20 — ATASCOSA LOOKOUT

Round trip 6 miles
Half day, allow 4 hours
Approx. elevations 4,700–6,255
Season all year, except after
snowstorms

This Forest Service lookout in the Atascosas is high enough to provide a good view of the southern Arizona grasslands and low enough to include considerable detail. Water is scarce or nonexistent along the trail, so be certain to carry a sufficient supply.

Take I-19 about 3 miles north of Nogales to the Pena Blanca-Ruby Road exit, which is State 289. Go west, past the Pena Blanca Lake turn-off, and when you have gone about 15 miles from I-19 (about 5 miles beyond Pena Blanca), some turnouts will be seen on the left. A sign is posted along the road designating "Trail" to help spot these turnouts. The trail, which is designated Trail #100, is not actively maintained and therefore rough in places.

The trail is easy to follow as it takes off across the road from the parking lot. It climbs somewhat parallel to the road for a while, passing through a landscape of grasses, ocotillos, agaves, and Mexican blue oaks against a backdrop of rolling hills.

After a quarter mile the trail goes through a gate on a little saddle. The elevation has changed so that junipers, Emory oaks, and Mexican pinyons are now common. The route gains elevation along the hillside, and other mountain ranges become visible to the east.

At about 1.5 miles there is a big, lichened rock formation above. Higher still, the trail swings around the hillside and continues gradually upward. Switchbacks begin about three quarters of a mile from the top, then the lookout is visible as the trail passes through a gate. The last short climb to the top is a series of steep, rock stairsteps.

Summit views include the Baboquivaris to the west and many small ranges in Mexico to the south. The Catalinas, Tanque Verdes, Rincons, and Santa Ritas lie to the northeast, and Nogales and Pena Blanca Lake are to the east.

Return by the same route.

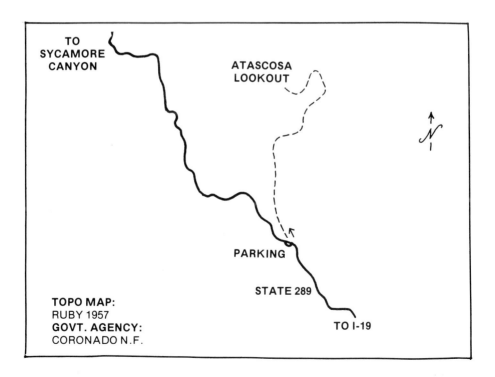

TO SYCAMORE CANYON

ATASCOSA LOOKOUT

N

PARKING

STATE 289

TO I-19

TOPO MAP:
RUBY 1957
GOVT. AGENCY:
CORONADO N.F.

21 — SYCAMORE CANYON

Round trip 12 miles
All day, allow 10 hours
Approx. elevations 4,000–3,500
Season all year

Desert canyons provide some of the Southwest's finest hiking environments. This hike is through a beautiful canyon filled with willows and sycamores and tenanted by some unusual and interesting wildlife. The hike ends at the Mexican border.

Take I-19 about 3 miles north of Nogales to the Pena Blanca-Ruby Road exit, which is State 289. Proceed about 10 miles and then bear left onto the Arivaca-Ruby Road, F.S. #39, continuing about 9 more miles to Sycamore Canyon Road, F.S. #218. Go left about 0.3 mile to a parking area at the Hank and Yank Historical Marker.

The trail is not too tough for the first mile, but then becomes very rocky and somewhat difficult as it goes in and out of the streambed. To get to the trailhead from the Hank and Yank parking area, walk past the adobe ruins, straight ahead on the dirt road and down to the creek bottom. There is no continuous trail—just a route downstream in the canyon where there are occasional trails of use. While this is a beautiful area, it would be unsafe if there was any likelihood of flash flooding.

The black and white birds that perch on twigs or rocks just above the water are black phoebes. The only fish to occur here is the Sonoran chub.

About a mile downstream, it is necessary to maneuver carefully around the righthand side over a cliff to avoid wading. Another half mile brings you to an area where you can work your way around the righthand side about five feet above the water. Be careful not to slip.

Not far beyond, continue straight ahead where a pretty little canyon comes in on the left. Bear Canyon soon enters on the left, and a fair trail of use develops along the lefthand side of the main canyon for a while.

Half a mile below Bear Canyon, look closely at the trees as you pass by. Epiphytic plants which look like sea urchins grow on the branches of some. Soon it is necessary to do a little wading where the steep, rocky sides prevent climbing around the creek channel.

As the elevation drops, the canyon walls recede. Mesquite becomes common in the canyon bottom, and saguaros appear on the hillsides. A barbed-wire fence stretched across the canyon indicates that you have reached the international boundary which is the turnaround point. Return by the same route.

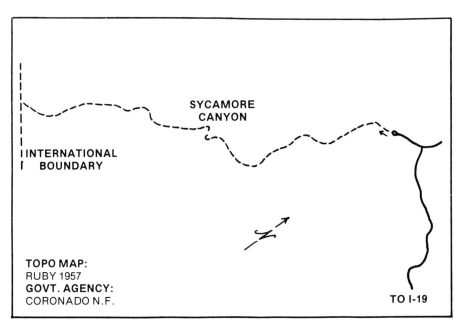

SYCAMORE CANYON

INTERNATIONAL BOUNDARY

TOPO MAP:
RUBY 1957
GOVT. AGENCY:
CORONADO N.F.

TO I-19

22 — BOG SPRINGS

Round trip 4.3 miles
Half day, allow 4 hours
Approx. elevations 5,100-6,600
Season all year except after snowstorms

Partly by old fire road, partly by trail, this hike loops through an interesting wooded area on the side of the Santa Rita Mountains. These mountains rise above some of Arizona's richest grasslands. In early summer the silvery green grass is liberally dotted with white prickle poppies and the pink and white "bottlebrushes" of a low-growing mimosa, making for a beautiful drive into the trailhead.

Take I-19 south from Tucson. A short distance beyond the Green Valley junction, turn east where a sign indicates Madera Canyon. Proceed about 13 miles through the grasslands to Madera Canyon where a sign indicates Bog Springs Campground. Turn left and proceed 0.5 mile into the campground. As you first enter the area, count the campsites on your right. The trail--actually a jeep road at this point--takes off just beyond the third campsite.

The first part of the hike follows the jeep trail through a woodland of silverleaf oaks, alligator junipers, Arizona white oaks, Emory oaks, Mexican pinyons, sotol and yuccas. An occasional sycamore grows in the wash, and flocks of noisy Mexican jays are common in this type of habitat.

Continue on the jeep road for 0.6 mile. A narrow forest trail takes off on the left here, marked by rock cairns on each side. There are several trails of use taking off to the left before the correct one. Look for a blaze mark on an oak. The road climbs steeply in the area of the junction, and the trail takes off on the left of the steep hill.

The route heads uphill, and the vegetation now includes netleaf oaks, Arizona madrones and nolina. After 0.7 mile on this route, the trail comes to Bog Springs. There are some nice views of Madera Canyon as the trail continues for 1.2 miles up to Kent Springs, leveling off somewhat as it nears the springs.

A two-track road drops steeply downhill from Kent Springs, eventually coming to a locked cable across the road. Not far beyond is a fork in the road. The righthand fork soon completes the loop and follows the road back to the campground.

Some hikers prefer to do this hike in reverse, making the steep climb to Kent Springs first.

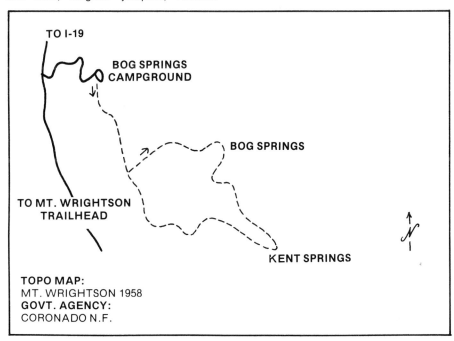

TO I-19

BOG SPRINGS
CAMPGROUND

BOG SPRINGS

TO MT. WRIGHTSON
TRAILHEAD

KENT SPRINGS

TOPO MAP:
MT. WRIGHTSON 1958
GOVT. AGENCY:
CORONADO N.F.

Meteor Crater

Seven Falls

Marshall Gulch below Aspen Trail

The Grand Canyon from head of Bright Angel Trail

Phoenix Mountain Preserve, South Mountain Park

Panoramic view in the Catalinas

Pima Canyon

Balanced rock

Bristlecone pine — Mount Humphreys

Spider Rock near White House Ruins

Prickly Pear Cactus Blossoms

Betatakin Ruins

23 — MOUNT WRIGHTSON

Round trip 16 miles
All day or backpack, allow 10 hours
Approx. elevations 5,400-9,500
Season May through October

As you look south from Tucson, Mount Wrightson is the dominant peak in the Santa Ritas. This hike begins in Madera Canyon, well known for its birdlife because a number of Mexican species just barely cross the border in this area. It is a long, strenuous hike from Madera Canyon to the summit of Mount Wrightson, but the views from the top and the challenge of getting there make it a favorite with veteran hikers.

From I-10 in Tucson, head south on I-19 toward Nogales. A short drive beyond Green Valley junction, turn east where a sign indicates Madera Canyon and continue about 13.5 miles to a fork in the road near the upper end of the canyon. Turn left into a parking lot here.

The trail takes off from the parking area, climbing through silverleaf oaks, Arizona white oaks, junipers, prickly pears, agaves, Arizona madrones and Emory oaks. There are sycamores and canyon grapes in the stream bottom.

At 4 miles is Josephine Saddle where there is a memorial to three Boy Scouts who perished in a snowstorm on November 15, 1958. Just before reaching the saddle, the trail passes Sprung Spring where there may be cool water.

Turn left in the saddle and, about 50 feet beyond, go to the left again. After another quarter mile of steep going, there is another trail fork. The trail to the left is the old, steep route up Wrightson; the route described here follows the newer trail which goes to the right. The telescope installation on Mount Hopkins can be seen from this point.

The trail continues to climb. At the 6-mile point, it swings around to the cooler north side of the mountain where netleaf oaks give way to pines and firs. About a mile beyond is the site of Baldy Cabin which burned down in the fall of 1973.

Half a mile above the cabin site, the trail tops a ridge. Turn left here to begin the long, steep half mile to the summit. Do not attempt this last part of the hike if there is ice on the trail.

Included in the view from the top are the Tucson Basin, the Catalina Mountains, the Tanque Verdes, the Rincons, the Huachucas, the town of Patagonia, Lake Patagonia, the Sierritas, the Baboquivaris and Madera Canyon.

Return by the same route.

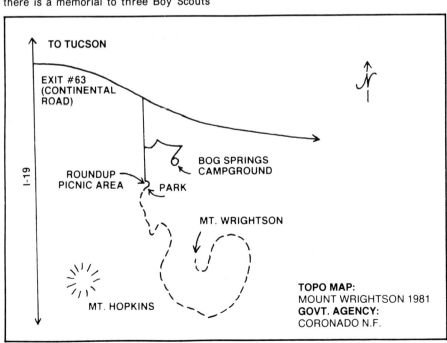

TO TUCSON

EXIT #63
(CONTINENTAL
ROAD)

I-19

ROUNDUP
PICNIC AREA

PARK

BOG SPRINGS
CAMPGROUND

MT. WRIGHTSON

MT. HOPKINS

TOPO MAP:
MOUNT WRIGHTSON 1981
GOVT. AGENCY:
CORONADO N.F.

24 — MILLER PEAK

Round trip 9.8 miles
All day or backpack, allow 10–12 hours
Approx. elevations 6,500–9,466
Season May through October

A stiff climb is the price of spectacular views from all along the Miller Peak Trail and from the lookout at the summit. Most of this trail climbs the sunny southern side of the Huachucas through rugged, relatively open country.

From Sierra Vista, take State 92 south to a sign indicating the turnoff to Coronado National Memorial. Continue past the visitor center at the memorial and up the winding dirt road to Montezuma Pass. Park here where there is a paved parking area.

At the time of this writing, the trailhead is situated on the north side of the road, 1,300 feet west of the pass. It may be moved back to the pass in the future but should be well signed if relocated.

The trail is the Crest Trail and is designated Trail #103. It takes off from the parking area and climbs immediately along grassy hillsides which offer good views of Sonora, Mexico. Vegetation along the trail includes Arizona white oak, Mexican pinyon, mountain mahogany, skunkbush sumac, flapjack prickly pear, and cane cholla.

At 1.4 miles the trail crosses the first of several mine tailings. Keep to the trail. The old shafts and drifts are unstable, and rattlesnakes are attracted to the cool, dark interiors.

As the trail continues to climb, alligator junipers become common. Higher up, Douglas firs, Gambel's Oaks, and occasional limber pines occur within the cooler contours of the canyons and north-facing slopes. Silverleaf oak, netleaf oak, and manzanita grow in the exposed hillsides and points. The fleshy agaves with the short, wide blades are Huachuca agaves. Fom some stretches of the trail, Miller Peak lookout can be seen—still a long climb away.

In a pretty, wooded area at 3.7 miles, Ash Canyon Trail diagonals downhill on the right. The main trail continues ahead.

There is a major trail junction at 4.4 miles. The left fork (Trail #103) continues to the Reef Road and Sawmill Canyon. You, however, should take the righthand fork, Trail #105, which climbs about 0.5 mile, via eight switchbacks, to the lookout. The trail goes through open fir forest and small, grassy meadows dotted with wildflowers in the summer. There are scattered thickets of Gambel's oak and aspen.

The trail ends at the lookout on a rocky summit at 4.9 miles. From an elevation of 9,466 feet, there is an unobscured view of the southwestern desert below. Several mountain ranges can be seen on a clear day, including the Patagonias, the Santa Ritas, and the Chiricahuas. The town of Sierra Vista can be seen edging down from the north, and a plume of smelter smoke rises from Cananea, Sonora, to the south. Nearer your feet are the scars left by the 1976 Carr Peak Fire.

Return by the same route.

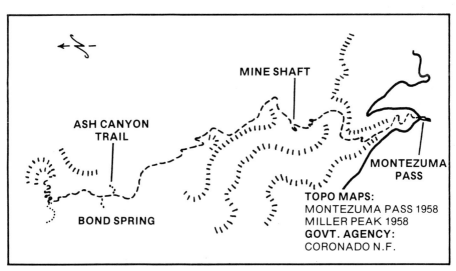

MINE SHAFT

ASH CANYON
TRAIL

MONTEZUMA
PASS

BOND SPRING

TOPO MAPS:
MONTEZUMA PASS 1958
MILLER PEAK 1958
GOVT. AGENCY:
CORONADO N.F.

25 — CORONADO PEAK

Round trip 7 miles
Half day, allow 5 hours
Approx. elevations 6,300-6,800
Season all year

Coronado National Memorial was set aside to commemorate the Francisco Vasquez de Coronado expedition of 1540 which passed through this general area in search of the legendary Seven Cities of Cibola. Coronado Peak is the highest point in the memorial.

From Sierra Vista, follow State 92 south to a sign indicating the turn-off to Coronado National Memorial, a unit of the National Park Service. Turn to the right and proceed 4.6 miles to parking at the visitor center.

Walk up the main road from the parking area for 0.1 mile to a road going to a picnic area. Joe's Canyon Trail to Coronado Peak starts at this road fork.

For the first half mile, the trail follows along the hillside in an area of grasses and oaks. Canyon grape is common in the vicinity of stream crossings.

The route continues uphill via switchbacks. Farther on, the hillside on the left is dominated by Mexican pinyons whereas oaks and grasses are more common on the southern exposure to the right. There are good views to the east from here.

After about 1.5 miles the trail reaches the top of the ridge and follows to the right. After another mile of more gradual climbing, the route drops off to the right-hand side of Coronado Peak. Wright's silktassel and cane cholla are two interesting plants growing along here; and the lookout on Miller Peak can be seen high above, 3 miles to the northwest.

The trail intersects an excellent interpretive trail which begins a short distance down the trail to the right. The summit is 0.3 mile up the hill. There are fine views from the top, including areas of Mexico to the south and some of Arizona's most beautiful grasslands.

Return is by the same route.

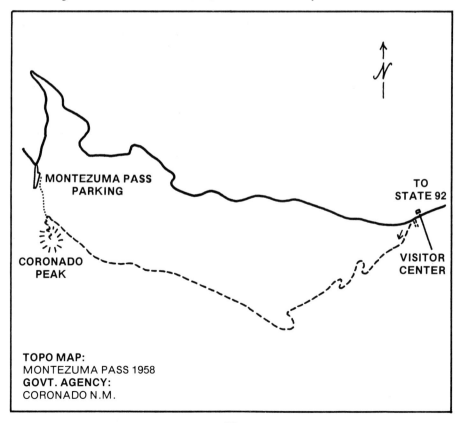

TOPO MAP:
MONTEZUMA PASS 1958
GOVT. AGENCY:
CORONADO N.M.

26 — COCHISE STRONGHOLD

Round trip 8.5 miles
All day, allow 7 hours
Approx. elevations 5,000–6,000
Season all year

It was in these mountains in 1872 that General O.O. Howard negotiated a peace treaty with Cochise, leader of the Chiricahua Apaches.

From I-10 southwest of Willcox, take U.S. 666 south and follow the signs for about 27 miles to Cochise Stronghold in the Dragoon Mountains. The last 9.5 miles is along Ironwood Road, a well maintained gravel road which goes west from 666. A Forest Service campground is at the road's end.

The well-maintained trail starts on the south side of the campground, following the left fork of a nature trail. At about 250 yards, the nature trail goes to the right; continue left on the Cochise Indian Trail which climbs through the East Stronghold. The trail is bordered by oaks, manzanitas, yuccas, junipers, madrones, and Mearn's sumac. Yarrow's spiny lizards bask on sun-warmed boulders along the trail.

As it continues, the route crosses the bed of a small stream that flows intermittently, depending on seasonal rains. A few sycamores and cottonwoods grow where their roots can reach permanent underground water.

A grassy area and a tumble-down fence at the 1-mile point make the area of Cochise Spring a pretty rest stop, although the spring is sometimes dry.

Half a mile farther, there are many interesting rock formations on the hillsides. It is easy to see how, once established, it would be difficult to surprise the Indians or engage them in open combat in terrain so well suited to their fighting style.

A few short switchbacks and three quarters of a mile bring you to Halfmoon Tank. This little catchment pond is bordered by cattails, and we saw several black-necked garter snakes sunning on pieces of floating wood.

Stronghold Divide is at 3 miles, the highest point on the hike and the division between east and west strongholds. This makes a suitable turn-around point if you prefer a less strenuous hike.

It is important that all hikers take plenty of water while hiking the Cochise Indian Trail. In fact, on a hot, dry, clear day, one full gallon is the minimum amount suggested. Hikers should not rely on finding good spring or creek water, unless advised by a Ranger.

The trail drops from the divide into the West Stronghold and proceeds for 1.75 miles of long switchbacks to a jeep road entering from the west. Part way down, Rincon Peak can be seen in the distance. There is a small creek (intermittent) lined with Arizona cypress, Arizona walnuts and sycamores near the road.

Return by the same route.

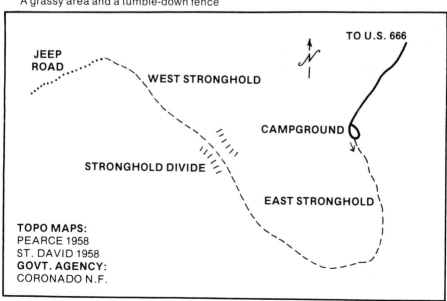

JEEP ROAD

WEST STRONGHOLD

TO U.S. 666

N

CAMPGROUND

STRONGHOLD DIVIDE

EAST STRONGHOLD

TOPO MAPS:
PEARCE 1958
ST. DAVID 1958
GOVT. AGENCY:
CORONADO N.F.

27 — FORT BOWIE

Round trip 3 miles
Part day, allow 3 hours
Approx. elevations 4,700–5,000
Season all year

In order for travelers to reach the precious water source at Apache Spring, it was necessary to enter Apache Pass, a narrow route between the Chiricahua and Dos Cabezas Mountains. The old Butterfield Overland Stage was routed through here, and many bloody skirmishes took place in the environs of the pass and the spring. Fort Bowie was established in 1862 to protect the water source at Apache Spring and was of strategic importance in the Indian campaigns until the surrender of Geronimo in 1886.

The only access to the site of the fort is by foot trail, situated midway in Apache Pass. There are two different ways to reach the trailhead, the first is to take Arizona 186 about 22 miles from Willcox to the graded dirt road leading east into Apache Pass. The second approach is to start in Bowie and take the well marked, graded road at the east end of town in a southerly direction about 12 miles.

The trailhead is in Apache Pass and is well marked. The entire trail is well documented with interpretive signs along the way, and they help to make the trek most interesting and informative. This historical site is a unit of the National Park Service, and all historic and natural objects are protected by law.

You will soon pass by an unidentified ruin, the ruins of the Butterfield Stage Station and the post cemetery. About half way to the fort, the trail crosses Siphon Canyon, a wide wash bordered by netleaf hackberries, desert willows, and Arizona walnuts. Grasses, Mesquites, and assorted cacti are the most common on the surrounding hills.

Apache Spring is on the left not far beyond. Its year-round water is now used by cattle and wildlife, but it is not safe for human consumption! Once the object of a life-or-death tug-of-war between troops and Indians, it is now just a pleasant rest stop along the trail.

The first Fort Bowie is on a little hill immediately south of the spring. As you approach the second Fort Bowie which was buit in 1868, notice all the sherds from broken beer bottles and other glassware. Most of this glass dates from the 1860s–1890s. Plan to take time to walk around the entire complex. A ranger is on duty at the small museum to answer questions.

Return by the same route, or choose the slightly steeper loop trail, as illustrated on the map.

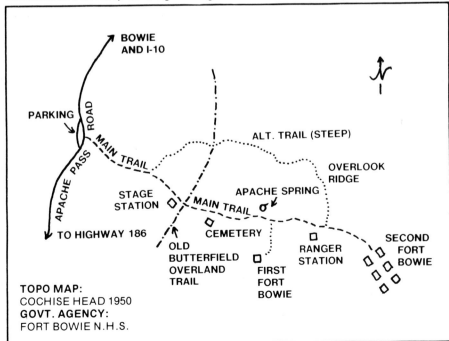

TOPO MAP:
COCHISE HEAD 1950
GOVT. AGENCY:
FORT BOWIE N.H.S.

28 — HEART OF ROCKS

Round trip 9.5 miles
All day, allow 7 hours
Approx. elevations 5,300-6,900
Season February through November

Chiricahua National Monument bristles with unusual rock formations, and this hike takes you among some of the most interesting.

Leave I-10 at Willcox and follow signs to the monument. The trailhead is at the upper end of the parking area at the visitor center.

The first 150 yards or so are on a self-guiding nature trail. Vegetation growing in the relatively dry valley includes canyon grape, silverleaf oak, skunkbush sumac, alligator juniper, poison ivy, Arizona white oak, Schott's yucca, Chihuahua pine, manzanita, nolina, Mearn's sumac, prickly pear and agave. The trail is wide and well defined.

The nature trail soon turns off to the left while the main trail continues ahead. A gradual climb soon affords a good view of numerous rock pinnacles on the opposite side of the canyon.

At 1.5 miles is a trail junction. Take the righthand fork (you will be coming back on the left). About three quarters of a mile beyond this junction, the trail passes along a hillside above a stand of Arizona cypress in a pretty little canyon.

Look for a big ponderosa snag on the left. Just to the right of it is a live pine riddled with thousands of holes made by acorn woodpeckers.

Near the third mile the trail switchbacks for a quarter mile into a rocky area. There is a trail junction here where the main trail continues ahead and a short trail goes left to the Heart of Rocks Loop Trail. This is a side trip worth taking, so go to the left. The loop begins almost immediately, going uphill to the left. Painted "footprints" conduct you around the 1-mile circuit which winds among some of the monument's most unusual rock formations.

When you arrive back at the main trail, turn to the left and continue a short distance to Big Balanced Rock. It has a diameter of 22 feet and an estimated weight of a thousand tons. The area along here is level for about a mile.

Where Inspiration Point Trail goes to the left, continue ahead on the main trail. It descends gradually for the next 1.5 miles. At Massai Point junction, continue ahead on the Echo Park-Headquarters Trail. A steady descent for another mile brings you to the canyon bottom. After a short climb you rejoin the trail you hiked up earlier in the day and re-hike the 1.5 miles to the parking area.

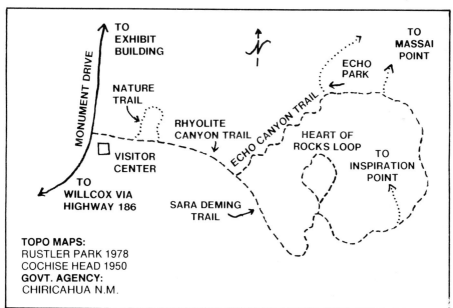

TOPO MAPS:
RUSTLER PARK 1978
COCHISE HEAD 1950
GOVT. AGENCY:
CHIRICAHUA N.M.

59

29 — NATURAL BRIDGE

Round trip 4.8 miles
Half day, allow 4 hours
Approx. elevations 5,522-6,000
Season February through November

Within the boundaries of Chiricahua National Monument lies some of the most beautiful and unusual country in the Southwest. This trail takes in an interesting cross-section of plants, animals and geological formations while working its way in to a natural bridge.

The monument is reached by taking State 186 from Willcox and following highway signs. An entrance fee is charged. Take the main monument road past the visitor center. The trailhead is beside the main road, not far beyond the campground entrance. There is a well-marked parking pullout on the left where the trail begins.

The route immediately drops down from the road and crosses the creekbed in Bonita Canyon. Among the trees here are Arizona cypress. They have scale-like leaves that resemble those of the juniper; however, the cypress is a tall, straight tree with vertically furrowed bark.

The trail climbs out of the creekbed and goes up Bonita Canyon about 500 feet before bending left up North Bonita Canyon. At 0.6 mile the trail pulls away from the bottom of North Bonita Canyon and climbs the hillside. As the vegetation thins out and the elevation increases, the view fans out over North Bonita and several other tree-filled canyons. The sides of the canyons are studded with tall rock columns and spires. Rufous-sided towhees and Yarrow's spiny lizards are common in this habitat.

At 0.9 mile the trail tops out on a plateau from which the lookout on Sugar Loaf Peak can be seen. The route across the plateau is gradually downhill through shrubs such as manzanita, shrub live oak and beargrass.

At 1.3 miles the trail drops into a canyon via several switchbacks. Silver-leaf oak, Arizona white oak, Mexican pinyon and alligator juniper are common in the pigmy forest of the canyon bottom. Shortly after crossing the creek here, there are some Arizona madrone trees-- not a common tree but easily identified by its rich red bark.

The trail proceeds down the canyon for a short distance, then swings left to cross Picket Park. The park is shaded by a mixed stand of Chihuahua and ponderosa pines.

The trail gradually ascends through the pines, crossing a small, sandy wash several times as it moves up a canyon. The canyon begins to narrow, and the trail climbs from the creek bottom at 2.2 miles and ends at a viewpoint at 2.4 miles.

It may take a minute to locate the bridge because it is well camouflaged among the cliffs and brush across the canyon. It is a squarish formation, twenty-six feet high and spanning thirty-seven feet across a small drainage.

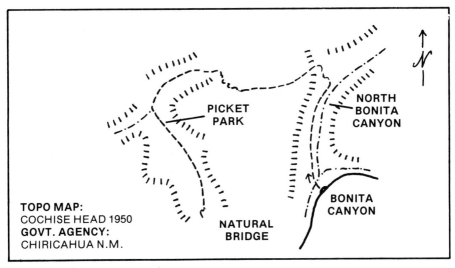

PICKET PARK

NORTH BONITA CANYON

BONITA CANYON

NATURAL BRIDGE

TOPO MAP:
COCHISE HEAD 1950
GOVT. AGENCY:
CHIRICAHUA N.M.

30 — ARCADIA TRAIL

Round trip 10.2 miles
All day, allow 8 hours
Approx. elevations 9,520–6,700
Season May through October

The Graham Mountains have long been a summer refuge for residents of Safford, but are far enough from major cities to be a little quieter than most big ranges. If the season is right, you might even have a chance at the wild raspberries along the trail between Shannon and Arcadia campgrounds. If you don't want to hike back up to the Shannon campground, you will have to have transportation arranged before starting out.

From I-10 take U.S. 666 north for about 25 miles to State 366. Turn west on 366 and proceed 21.8 miles to the road going to Shannon campground on the right. You will pass by Arcadia campground enroute. Continue 0.3 mile to the trailhead on the righthand side of the Shannon campground loop road. The Arcadia Trail is part of the National Recreation Trail System, and is designated Trail #328.

Shortly beyond the Trailhead, the trail passes through a relatively open logging area where wild raspberries are common. Beyond is a cool forest of Douglas fir, Englemann spruce, and quaking aspen. The forest floor is strewn with last year's leaves and downed timber. There are several slides of angular, lichen-covered rocks in this area.

At 0.7 mile the trail starts to switchback, climbing steadily through a large stand of aspens. It tops out near some huge boulders in a little saddle at 1.1 miles. Now it drops down about 40 feet to a trail junction where a side trail climbs to Heliograph Peak. Arcadia Trail continues downhill. In general, the rest of the route is through drier, more open forest with an occasional panoramic view of distant valleys and ridges.

The trail wanders in and out of the shade as it diagonals down the steep slopes of Heliograph Peak. Douglas fir gradually yields to Gambel's oak and ponderosa pine. Also look for the large, distinctive cones of the limber pine. In fact, it is possible to identify the common trees here simply by studying the needles, cones, and leaves at your feet. Where the route swings out onto hot, exposed points, netleaf and silverleaf oaks occur.

There is a trail junction at 3.1 miles. The lefthand fork is Noon Creek Ridge Trail. Take the righthand fork which continues downhill toward Arcadia via a number of long switchbacks. There is an occasional view of the campground and the main road below. Unfortunately there is also a view of the defunct Swift Trail Road— an idiots' delight that, so far, hasn't panned out or done anything to enhance the appearance of the land.

The trail crosses a drainage bottom at 4.7 miles. Bigtooth maples, Douglas firs, limber pines, inland boxelders, and violets congregate here where there is usually a thin trickle of water coming down the steep gorge.

At 5.1 miles the hike ends at a picnic area just above Arcadia campground. From here it is a short hike out to the main road.

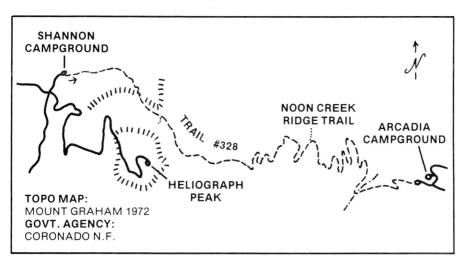

SHANNON
CAMPGROUND

NOON CREEK
RIDGE TRAIL

ARCADIA
CAMPGROUND

TRAIL #328

HELIOGRAPH
PEAK

TOPO MAP:
MOUNT GRAHAM 1972
GOVT. AGENCY:
CORONADO N.F.

31 — WHITE HOUSE RUINS

Round trip 2.5 miles
Part day, allow 2 hours
Approx. elevations 6,200–5,600
Season all year except after storms

Throughout these beautiful canyons are the ruins of prehistoric pueblo Indians. Some of the earliest sites date back to about 350 A.D., but the larger cliff dwellings were built between 1100 and 1300. White House was begun in 1060 A.D., with at least some work being done as late as 1275 A.D.

From State 191 near the town of Chinle, take the signed road to Canyon de Chelly National Monument. Drive 2.7 miles to the visitor center for an interpretation of the area and its people, then drive 5 miles east and turn left toward White House Overlook. The parking area is 0.6 mile from the turn-off.

White House Ruins can be seen in the cliff far below the overlook. The Rio de Chelly winds through the canyon bottom, bordered by cottonwoods and Navajo farms. It may or may not be running.

Hike to the right from the overlook and follow the canyon rim at a safe distance for about a quarter mile to the signed trailhead. Turn left and go through the gate and tunnel in the rock.

The trail switchbacks down interesting cliffs of sandstone which were once sand dunes. The bands of sand still show as clearly as when they were formed.

As the trail begins to level off near the canyon bottom, it passes through a tunnel about 80 feet long. Framed by the far end of the tunnel is a brush corral and stock shelter. This Navajo farm is private property; do not trespass or photograph. As you emerge from the tunnel, you also see the hogan against a backdrop of red sandstone cliffs.

Shortly after leaving the tunnel, the trail turns left and goes downstream. You may have to do some wading at this point as the ruins are across the river a short distance ahead.

The ruins are tucked into a horizontal cleft in the sandstone about seventy feet above the river bed. There are more ruins at the base and a few pictographs on the sandstone. At one time there were about eighty rooms in these dwellings, housing perhaps a hundred people.

Return by the same route.

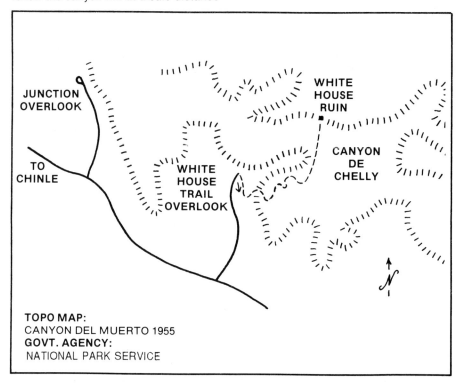

JUNCTION OVERLOOK

WHITE HOUSE RUIN

TO CHINLE

WHITE HOUSE TRAIL OVERLOOK

CANYON DE CHELLY

N

TOPO MAP:
CANYON DEL MUERTO 1955
GOVT. AGENCY:
NATIONAL PARK SERVICE

32 — PETRIFIED FOREST

Round trip 4 miles
Half day, allow 5 hours
Approx. elevations 5,800–5,500
Season all year

This hike enters an area where there are a number of large petrified logs. With luck, you may be able to work your way in to Onyx Bridge which is a petrified log fifty feet long. This hike will serve as an introduction to the desolate but interesting back country of Petrified Forest National Park.

If you plan to spend the night, it is necessary to obtain a wilderness permit from the park visitor center. Permits are not required for day hikers, however, as long as they leave by the posted closing time. A brief check with the ranger on duty may be helpful to all hikers in regard to getting up to the minute trail information. All petrified wood and other minerals are completely protected, so please do not try to collect anything within the park. Specimens can be obtained from stores in the area which sell petrified wood collected outside the park.

Proceed from the visitor center to the parking area at Kachina Point which is in the northern part of the park. The trail takes off from the left side of the Painted Desert Inn. It is possible with binoculars (but not always easy) to see Onyx Bridge from here. Carefully identify prominent landmarks before starting out.

Take the switchbacks to the bottom of the hill behind the inn and then head to Lithodendron Wash. Once in the bottom of the wash, which is the lowest part where the main channel of water will flow after a rainstorm, turn right and proceed upstream about 0.3 mile to where the trail will be seen exiting on the opposite bank. The wash is relative barren except for mud cracks, scattered grasses and various annual plants. The Painted Desert Inn is visible from behind you and serves as a landmark for orientation.

To find the elusive Onyx Bridge, study the map carefully. Proceed to a point just before you would reach a somewhat rounded, reddish cliff ("C" on map). A side canyon goes to the left just before this formation. Hike up this small canyon for 300 yards to Onyx Bridge—which remains elusive at this point. There are a number of large pieces of petrified wood in this side canyon. Keep to the bottom, righthand side until you come to an overhang which prevents further progress. At this point you are only 40 feet from the bridge. Now hike back down the canyon a very short distance to where there is a fork. Go up this fork a short distance, keeping in mind the bridge's position in relation to the overhang.

Onyx Bridge is light tan in color and two to three feet in diameter. It is about three feet above the ground in the middle and is very fragile. Please view it from a respectful distance. If you wish to explore in the area, keep track of the Painted Desert Inn, thereby keeping your bearings for the return hike.

Return is by the same route.

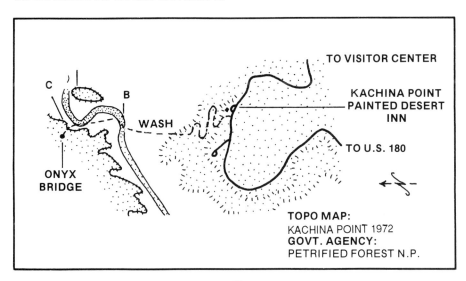

TOPO MAP:
KACHINA POINT 1972
GOVT. AGENCY:
PETRIFIED FOREST N.P.

33 — RAINBOW BRIDGE

Round trip 26 miles
Backpack, allow 3 days
Approx. elevations 6,400–3,600
Season April through October

Rainbow Bridge is the world's largest natural bridge, and the hike into it is long, rough, oftentimes hot—and very rewarding. A permit is required to hike the trail and it can be obtained by contacting Recreational Resources Department, The Navajo Tribe, P.O. Box 308, Window Rock, AZ 86515. The trail (and the route to the trailhead) goes through isolated country where help is generally a long distance away. It must be emphasized that only the experienced hiker should even consider making this hike and that gasoline may not be available locally. You should also take sufficient water, since none is available along the trail.

Take State 98 to a dirt road leading to Inscription House and Navajo Mountain. (This turn-off is 52 miles southeast of the town of Page and 14 miles northwest of U.S. 160.) Follow the dirt road past Inscription House Trading Post for 35 miles from State 98 to a sign at a road junction. The main road continues to the right to Navajo Mountain Trading Post. Take the lefthand fork and proceed 5.2 miles, then turn right onto a dirt road marked by a single 12-foot juniper which has been carved with the initials "IM." The ruins of the old Rainbow Lodge are about 1.6 miles in on this road. Because of the road's poor condition, it may be necessary to park your vehicle and hike part of the way.

Hike uphill from the lodge, watching for the trailhead. It is marked by a tall rock cairn, and the trail takes off to the left.

There are milepost markers along the entire route. In the first 5 miles, the trail drops into and out of four steep canyons, following along the southwest side of Navajo Mountain. Pinyon and juniper are the dominant vegetation.

Yabut Pass is at the 5-mile point. From the pass, the trail plunges 1,600 feet to the bottom at Cliff Canyon, a distance of 2 miles. The next 2 are more gradual as the route continues down the canyon, passing the First Water campsite near the 8-mile point. Farther downstream at about 9 miles, the trail leaves Cliff Canyon and cuts to the right. The towering sandstone cliffs close in on the trail as it climbs to Redbud Pass at 9.4 miles. The route drops down from the pass to the 10-mile point, and the next 2 miles are more or less along a creek. The canyon walls are red sandstone streaked with desert varnish, and there is a lush growth of cottonwoods, Gambel's oaks and redbuds in the canyon bottom.

Just beyond the 12-mile point is a gate, and Echo Camp is on the righthand side a short distance ahead. At 13 miles is Rainbow Bridge, shaped just as the name implies, seemingly as large, and just as beautiful in its own way.

Return is by the same route.

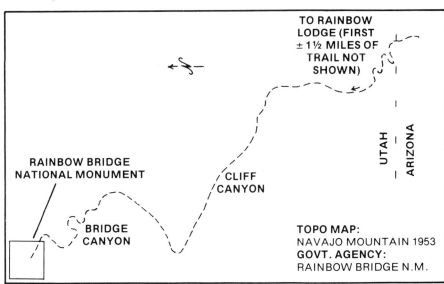

TO RAINBOW LODGE (FIRST ± 1½ MILES OF TRAIL NOT SHOWN)

UTAH | ARIZONA

RAINBOW BRIDGE NATIONAL MONUMENT

CLIFF CANYON

BRIDGE CANYON

TOPO MAP:
NAVAJO MOUNTAIN 1953
GOVT. AGENCY:
RAINBOW BRIDGE N.M.

34 — KEET SEEL RUINS

Round trip 16 miles
All day, allow 9 hours
Approx. elevations 7,200–6,300
Season determined by
  National Park Service

Keet Seel is the largest and best preserved of all cliff dwellings in Arizona, In order to maintain this magnificent monument to North American history, the number of visitors is strictly regulated, and a permit to visit the ruins must be obtained in advance from the Chief Ranger at Navajo National Monument. At the time of publication, the ruin is only open to hikers 3 days a week—Friday, Saturday and Sunday, starting on Memorial Day weekend and ending just after the Labor Day weekend. It is strongly suggested that you contact the Chief Ranger at least two months before making the hike to assure obtaining a permit.

To get there from U.S. 160, turn north where signs indicate Navajo National Monument. Proceed 9 miles to the visitor center for directions to the trailhead and to verify your permit. You must be on the trail by 9:00 a.m. on the day of your hike, and if you wish to tour the ruins, you must be there before 3:30 p.m. A trail guide is available, for a small fee, at the visitor center, and purchasing one helps make the trek more enjoyable.

From the visitor center, the hike begins about 1.5 miles back toward Betatakin Canyon, and your permit must be presented at the trailhead before starting out. The trail begins with a walk of about one mile from the new trailhead parking area to a series of switchbacks which descend into the valley below. Dark green juniper and pinyons against the red sandstone makes this a very pretty stretch of trail.

Heavy sheep traffic obscures any definite trail in the valley, and the route is indicated by marked posts. It goes upstream through the second drainage coming in from the left after you reach the valley. There is a hogan off to the right, and sheep dogs will probably create a disturbance if they are around.

You may have to do some wading as you hike up the creek bottom for about a mile to a fork in the canyon. The route follows the left fork upstream along a sandy bench to the right of a little falls before dropping back to the creek bottom. It continues upstream for several miles to another waterfall.

There is a switchback to the right around the falls. The route continues up the creek, sometimes along the creek bottom, sometimes along a sandy bench on the righthand side about 50 feet above the water. If you loose the trail, keep in mind that the route is generally upstream. Be very careful through here, and watch for quicksand!

After a third falls, there is a fair trail along the righthand bench. Keet Seel is on the left side of the canyon a short distance upstream from the camping area. Camping is primitive here and there is not potable water available, so be sure to be properly prepared. Remember, YOU CAN NOT ENTER THE RUINS WITHOUT A RANGER!

Potsherds, arrowheads, yucca-fiber ropes, animal bones and tiny corncobs still lie where the Indians left them almost 700 years ago. The soot on the walls appears as recent as last night's campfire. Please do not touch any thing.

Return by the same route.

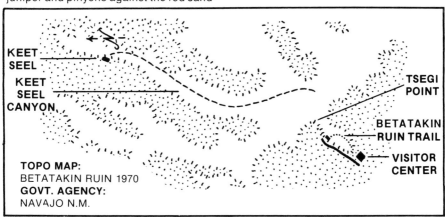

KEET SEEL

KEET SEEL CANYON

TSEGI POINT

BETATAKIN RUIN TRAIL

VISITOR CENTER

TOPO MAP:
BETATAKIN RUIN 1970
GOVT. AGENCY:
NAVAJO N.M.

35 — METEOR CRATER

Round trip 2.6 miles
Part day, allow 3 hours
Approx. elevations 5,640–5,740
Season all year, cold in winter

Some 49,000 years ago a gigantic meteorite weighing an estimated 1.7 million tons smashed into the northern Arizona plateau, burying itself approximately 600 feet below the bottom of a crater 570 feet deep. This hike circles the world's most famous meteor crater.

The crater is reached by taking I-40 about 36 miles east from Flagstaff or about 12 miles west from Winslow to Meteor Crater Road. Follow the road for about 6 miles south to the crater. An entrance fee is charged, but it is worthwhile even if you just tour the museum without hiking the trail.

From the side of the museum that faces the crater, take the paved path going left for 130 yards to a viewing area. There are good views from here and from many points along the hike, both of the crater and the surrounding plains. The San Francisco Peaks are visible to the west.

Keep in mind before you start out that this hike should not be made if an electrical storm is brewing. The hike is entirely on a well marked and recently improved trail, with 8 numbered signs along the way indicating particular points of interest. In addition, an informative rim trail guide is provided to all those choosing to take the trek. The trail starts at the viewing area and generally follows the crater rim. The upper, inside walls of the crater are precipitous and there are places where hikers should be careful not to get too close to the edge.

The sparse vegetation includes many small shrubs such as four-wing saltbush, yucca and Mormon tea. There are scattered stands of windswept junipers and Colorado pinyons. There are some patches of fine sand along the trial where you may be able to identify the tracks of birds, insects, lizards and small mammals. Cottontail rabbits and antelope ground squirrels are common in the area. Rock wrens bounce about the rim, and an occasional hawk wheels over the crater.

There are several places along the route where there is evidence of old mining activities—cuts in the crater rim, iron wheels, concrete, large timbers, windlasses, old rope and related relics. In 1904, a mining company founded by Daniel M. Barringer drilled in various areas of the crater. Water, quicksand and the devastating effects of the hard meteorite material on the drill bits made mining impractical. Old rusting machinery, planks, etc., are still scattered over the bottom of the crater.

At 1.2 and 1.3 miles, several old cabins can be seen to the left of the trail. There are a number of quarries in the vicinity. At 1.5 miles there are remnants of an old rock building to the left of the trail. At 2.2 miles there are the ruins of a rock house with a chimney and storage cellar. (Just before reaching these ruins, the route splits into two trails which rejoin near the ruin.) Next to the ruin is a clearing from which a two-track road heads toward the museum, soon narrowing down to a trail. Back at the museum, walk along the left side of the building to its entrance and the end of the hike at 2.6 miles.

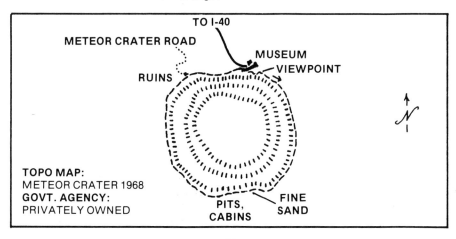

TO I-40

METEOR CRATER ROAD

MUSEUM
VIEWPOINT

RUINS

TOPO MAP:
METEOR CRATER 1968
GOVT. AGENCY:
PRIVATELY OWNED

PITS,
CABINS

FINE
SAND

N

36 — ARAVAIPA CANYON

Round trip 10 miles
All day or backpack
Allow 8 hours
Approx. elevations 2,600–2,800
Season all year, water cold in winter

This beautiful canyon was carved by Aravaipa Creek which has its source high in the Galiuro Mountains. It is a rare thing in Arizona—a canyon where the water still runs all year. The margins of the creek are crowded by ash trees, cottonwoods and willow thickets, and the sides of the canyon bristle with stands of saguaro cacti and other desert plants.

You must obtain a hiking permit from the Bureau of Land Management in Safford (see address under "Government Agencies") prior to entering Aravaipa Canyon Primitive Area. The number of hikers who may use the area at a given time is limited in order to protect both resources and solitude. Aravaipa Canyon is not a place to hunt, nor would hunting be safe here.

From the town of Mammoth, drive north about 8.4 miles on State 77 to Aravaipa Road. Turn right and proceed east for 11.8 miles to where you enter private property owned by the Nature Conservancy. Park here and walk over to the creek a short distance beyond.

The route now follows Aravaipa Creek upstream and involves a considerable amount of wading. The entire route follows the canyon bottom, making countless crossings from one side to the other. Trails of use firm up and fade, washed out by water, obscured by lush growth or disappearing among the rocks. Just follow the creek.

Even experienced hikers disagree on what is the best footwear for this hike. Old tennis shoes are a favorite, but you should plan on removing them several times to dump out sand and gravel. Boots are really not suitable here, nor would this be a very comfortable hike during cold winter months.

A wide variety of birds nest along Aravaipa, and seven species of native fish occur in its waters. The large fish you see most often are mountain suckers.

About 5 miles upstream is a large side canyon entering on the left. This is Horse Camp Canyon and makes a good turnaround point for the day hiker. Backpackers will find a number of suitable campsites in this area.

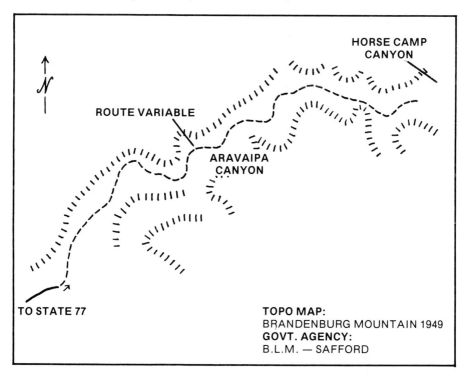

HORSE CAMP CANYON

ROUTE VARIABLE

ARAVAIPA CANYON

TO STATE 77

TOPO MAP:
BRANDENBURG MOUNTAIN 1949
GOVT. AGENCY:
B.L.M. — SAFFORD

37 — PINE MOUNTAIN

Round trip 9.5 miles
All day, allow 7 hours
Approx. elevations 5,080–6,814
Season May through October

The Pine Mountain Wilderness, while not large, is quiet and off the beaten track. The views from the Verde Rim and Pine Mountain offer unobstructed panoramas of range upon range of ridges and valleys, without a city in sight. Be advised that there is no potable water available anywhere along this route, so be sure to take a sufficient supply with you. In addition, it is recommended that you carry insect repellent in your supplies.

To get to the trailhead, go about 6 miles north of Cordes Junction on Interstate 17, and exit on the Dugas-Orme offramp. Proceed east on Dugas Road (Forest Service Road #68) about 19 miles to the Salt Flat camping area, following the signs to Pine Mountain. Parking and camping is available at Salt Flat.

An old road goes to the right from the camping area and immediately crosses a creek, shortly thereafter becoming Trail #159. From there, follow the signs to Willow Springs and the Double T Ranch.

At 0.6 miles is the Nelson Place. There are still a few apple trees here and some rambling remains of old rock walls. Nelson Place Spring is to the right, about 200 feet ahead.

The route continues upstream, crossing the usually dry bed of Beehive Canyon at 0.8 mile. The creek is crossed several times as the trail works its way up to Willow Springs junction, at 2.6 miles, where an old concrete tank can be seen on the left. Take the righthand fork, which is still Trail #159, and climb rather steeply along the hillside. You will be returning via the lefthand fork. The "Clover Leaf," the next major junction, is encountered at the 3.1 mile mark. There, you should bear left onto Trail #14 as it climbs up the ridge through the trees.

Continue 1.2 more miles to where Trail #14 intersects the Verde Rim Trail (Trail #161), and bear left.

Common trees in the more sheltered areas include oaks, ponderosa pines and an occasional large alligator juniper. Agaves, prickly pear, mountain mahogany, yuccas, and beargrass grow on the more exposed slopes along and below the Verde Rim.

At 4.9 miles a sign points to a short trail which climbs to the top of Pine Mountain, on the right. Views are superb from there, and there is also a summit register. Actually this is only a high point along the ridge. The main trail continues ahead from the summit junction, soon descending via a series of steep switchbacks to where it meets Trail #12, at 5.3 miles. Head downhill, to the left, from here. Trail #12 descends steadily, more or less parallel to the bottom of the drainage, and crosses the small creekbed from time to time.

The route continues down to Willow Springs junction, at 6.8 miles, and, from there, proceeds downhill and back to the trailhead, ending at 9.5 miles.

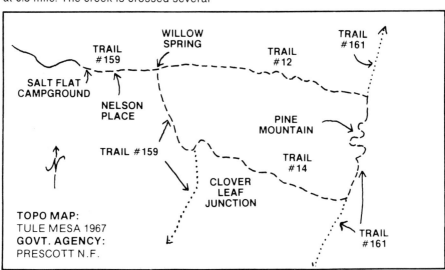

TOPO MAP:
TULE MESA 1967
GOVT. AGENCY:
PRESCOTT N.F.

38 — MAZATZAL PEAK

Round trip 17 miles
All day or backpack, allow 12 hours
Approx. elevations 4,000–6,500
Season May through October

This long and tough hike goes completely around rugged Mazatzal Peak, situated a short distance southwest of Rye. To get to the trailhead, go south from town 1.4 miles on Highway 87 to the bridge crossing Rye Creek. From there, continue 0.1 mile, turn right onto Forest Service Road 419, and proceed 4.8 miles to road's end.

The hike begins on the Barnhardt trail (Trail #43), which passes through a fence as it takes off from the upper end of the parking area. Junipers, Arizona white oaks, Emory oaks, agaves, nolina and sotol grow in this rather dry area. The Mazatzal Wilderness boundary is about one mile from the start.

The trend is uphill for the first 1.5 miles, but is relatively gradual. The route then begins a long series of rocky switchbacks, often swinging into cool recesses where there are shade trees, running water and occasional little pools. Ponderosa pine, Arizona walnut, sycamore and velvet ash are common in these areas.

The trek continues to a junction at 4.9 miles. The Sandy Saddle Trail (Trail #231) takes off to the right toward Horsecamp Seep, but you should continue straight on the Barnhardt Trail. The next mile is relatively level and passes through an old burn.

At the next junction, about 6 miles from the start, turn left onto Mazatzal Divide Trail (Trail #23) toward Windsor Spring. There is another junction 400 yards farther along. Keep left, staying on Trail #23. The route is overgrown in spots but not very difficult to follow. When you come to Brody Seep junction, continue straight ahead on the Mazatzal Divide Trail. Water can sometimes be obtained at Brody Seep, about one mile below.

This part of the trail is marked with rock cairns and becomes better defined as it runs along a dry, rocky hillside. You are now on the opposite side of Mazatzal Peak and will gradually climb to a piney ridge. Turn left at the trail junction on the ridge.

The journey continues downhill and intersects the Y Bar Basin Trail (Trail #44), approximately 9.5 miles from the starting point. Windsor Spring is just below here. Shortly thereafter the trail angles upward, rather steeply, for a mile to a divide.

From the divide, you will drop through a forest several miles, and there will be many spectacular views along the way. The final stretch is very rocky, and ends at the parking area where the hike began.

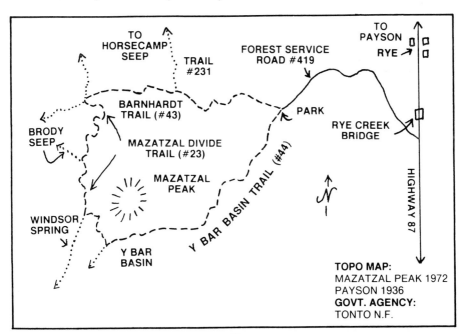

TO HORSECAMP SEEP

TRAIL #231

FOREST SERVICE ROAD #419

TO PAYSON

RYE

PARK

BARNHARDT TRAIL (#43)

BRODY SEEP

MAZATZAL DIVIDE TRAIL (#23)

RYE CREEK BRIDGE

MAZATZAL PEAK

Y BAR BASIN TRAIL (#44)

WINDSOR SPRING

Y BAR BASIN

HIGHWAY 87

TOPO MAP:
MAZATZAL PEAK 1972
PAYSON 1936
GOVT. AGENCY:
TONTO N.F.

39 — GROOM CREEK

Round trip 9 miles
Half day, allow 6 hours
Approx. elevations 6,300–7,700
Season May through October

This is a pretty hike, particularly the return along South Spruce Ridge. The open forest seems to be inhabited by more wildlife than we've come to expect on a hike so near populated areas.

From East Gurley in dowtown Prescott, turn south on Senator Highway. This junction is about three-quarters of a mile west of the junction of State 69 and U.S. 89. Six miles south of town, park on the left side of the highway where the Groom Creek Loop Trail begins (F.S. Trail #307).

The route is well used and begins to climb immediately. Keep an eye out for blaze marks on the trees. Ponderosa pines grow on the hillsides, with Douglas firs coming in higher up.

At the Camp Wamatochick junction, the hike we're describing continues straight ahead (left). Shortly beyond is another junction where it continues straight toward Spruce Mountain Lookout. There is a long series of switchbacks between this junction and a picnic area where a road comes in from the other side. It is about a hundred yards up to the lookout from the picnic area if you want to take in a good view of Prescott.

From the picnic area, continue to the right watching for blaze marks. The trail follows the ridge for more than a mile and is generally level. There are some pleasant, cool areas along here. As it continues, the trail passes some old mine shafts and test holes.

The last part of the hike is mainly level or downhill among Gambel's oaks, pines and junipers. There are several dirt roads which the trail crosses as it passes through an area which has been logged over and thinned.

At the Senator Highway, turn to the right and walk north for about half a mile to the trailhead.

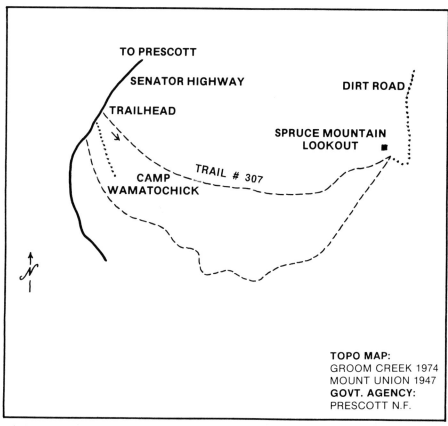

TOPO MAP:
GROOM CREEK 1974
MOUNT UNION 1947
GOVT. AGENCY:
PRESCOTT N.F.

40 — GRANITE MOUNTAIN

Round trip 7.7 miles
Half day, allow 6 hours
Approx. elevations 5,800–7,000
Season May through October

This rugged, pine-clad ridge affords fine views of the city of Prescott and the surrounding forest. The area is popular with rock climbers, and it may be possible to watch a climb on the rock face above the lower part of the trail. A pair of binoculars would be a handy item to have on this hike.

From the intersection of Gurley and Montezuma next to the courthouse in Prescott, head west on Gurley for 0.3 mile to Grove Avenue. Turn to the right and proceed for 1.1 miles to Iron Springs Road and proceed west for 2.9 miles, then turn to the right towards Granite Basin Recreation Area. Continue for 3.1 miles to a road fork. The righthand fork goes to Granite Basin Lake, but you should continue straight ahead for another 0.9 mile to the end of the road.

The Granite Mountain Trail, F.S. Trail #261, begins here, a gravelly path that climbs rather gradually as it follows along a small wash. At 1.5 miles there is a trail junction in Blair Pass; take the righthand fork. The trail climbs steadily from the pass to Granite Mountain Saddle via a number of switchbacks. About 0.5 miles from the saddle, you will see granite boulders over 1.7 billion years old. Manzanita, mountain mahogany, sotol, single-leaf pinyon, agave and nolina are all common in this area.

When you reach Granite Mountain Saddle, turn to the right. The trail continues to climb for a while, then passes over a relatively level area of scattered ponderosa pines and huge boulders. From the saddle, it is a mile to the viewpoint where the hike ends. Granite Basin Lake is included in the view below.

Return by the same route.

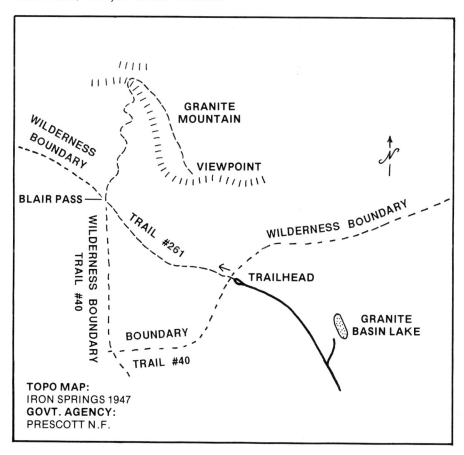

TOPO MAP:
IRON SPRINGS 1947
GOVT. AGENCY:
PRESCOTT N.F.

41 — THUMB BUTTE

Round trip 2.3 miles
Part day, allow 2 hours
Approx. elevations 5,700–6,500
Season April through November

Thumb Butte is a rocky little point jutting above the forest near Prescott. The short hike to its top makes a pleasant outing, both for the exercise and the opportunity to view Prescott from above.

From the intersection of Gurley and Montezuma next to the courthouse in Prescott, head west on Gurley which will soon become Thumb Butte Road. At a distance of 3.1 miles from the courthouse, the road enters Prescott National Forest. Continue another 0.2 mile and park on the left where Thumb Butte Trail begins.

The trail climbs easily for almost a mile.

Ponderosa pines are common along here, sharing the landscape with three kinds of oak—Gambel's oak which has deeply lobed deciduous leaves, Emory oak which is the other tree-sized oak, and shrub live oak which is low growing as the name implies. The vegetation gradually changes to junipers, prickly pears, pinyons and garrya as the trail gains the exposed ridge.

At 1.1 miles is a junction. The left fork climbs to the base of Thumb Butte. To reach the summit would involve a climb of 200 feet of steep cliffs and is not recommended. The righthand fork goes about 150 yards to a vista point from which there are good views of Prescott and the San Francisco Peaks.

The trail loops back down the slope on steep switchbacks to the starting point.

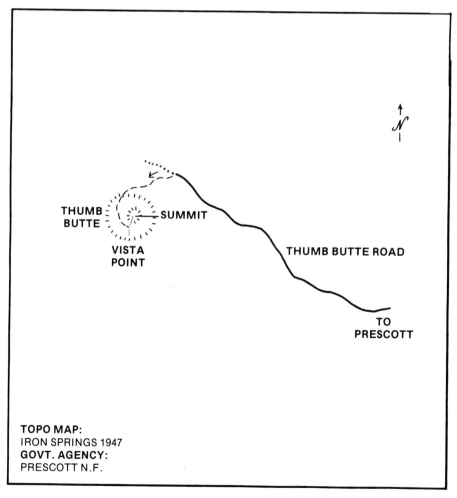

THUMB
BUTTE — SUMMIT

VISTA
POINT

THUMB BUTTE ROAD

TO
PRESCOTT

TOPO MAP:
IRON SPRINGS 1947
GOVT. AGENCY:
PRESCOTT N.F.

42 — EAST POCKET

Round trip 2.8 miles
Part day, allow 3.5 hours
Approx. elevations 5,200-6,800
Season May through September

This is a relatively short but steep hike from Oak Creek to the Mogollon Rim and offers fine views of the surrounding mesa country and parts of the canyon below.

From the junction of State 179 and U.S. 89A in Sedona, drive north for 8.4 miles on 89A to Bootlegger Campground which is on the left between highway mileposts 383 and 384. **NOTE:** This campground is occasionally closed. When planning this hike, keep in mind that it is impossible to cross the creek to the trailhead if the water is high.

Near the south end of the campground are some stairs going down to the creek. Wade across, then walk uphill a short distance to a well-used trail paralleling the creek. About 100 yards up this trail is another trail cutting diagonally uphill. This is the East Pocket Trail (also called the A. B. Young Trail).

The trail is steep and switchbacks all the way to the top. Douglas firs, ponderosa pines and oaks dominate the streamside vegetation, but these soon relinquish the landscape to plants such as shrub live oak, yucca, mountain mahogany and Wright's silktassel. White-throated swifts often wing overhead.

The main trail ends at the ridge where you can rest and savor the view before returning by the same route.

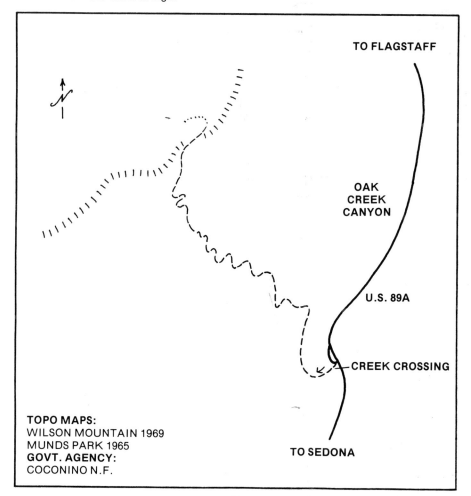

TO FLAGSTAFF

OAK CREEK CANYON

U.S. 89A

CREEK CROSSING

TO SEDONA

TOPO MAPS:
WILSON MOUNTAIN 1969
MUNDS PARK 1965
GOVT. AGENCY:
COCONINO N.F.

43 — WEST FORK

Round trip 6 miles
All day, allow 6 hours
Approx. elevations 5,300–5,600
Season May through October

This is a beautiful canyon with running water that is more reminiscent of scenery in Montana or Canada than Arizona. Fortunately for West Fork, the Forest Service has set it aside as a "Research Natural Area."

From the junction of State 179 and U.S. 89A in Sedona, drive north 9.8 miles on 89A to parking on the righthand side of the road between highway mileposts 384 and 385. Cross the road and Oak Creek to what is left of the Mayhews Lodge which burned down in 1980. Very little is left of the lodge except a rock fireplace and a few foundation walls, but it serves as a landmark for the trailhead. Follow the trail, which is F.S. Trail #1-8, past the remnants of the lodge into the canyon. The route crosses the stream a number of times. If the water is too deep or too cold at the first crossing, save this hike for another time because conditions will become more severe farther in. Keep in mind that thunder showers can also raise the water level in a very short period of time.

Ponderosa pines grow on the steep sides of the canyon, alternating with cliffs of red or light pink sandstone. Douglas firs, bigtooth maples and Gambel's oak grow out of the lush tangle of shrubbery in the canyon bottom. Ferns, equisetum (horsetail) and wildflowers are common. The clumps of grass-like plants seen growing in the streambed are sedges.

Care should be taken in wading; the sandstone has a tendency to become slick from the growth of algae. The route is not always marked, and after about 3.0 miles of well-trod trail, there are only occasional trails of use. The route continues to follow near or in the streambed.

We have not designated any particular turn-around point, but at about 2.5 miles is a place where the stream has cut into the sides of both banks to form a little overhang. This makes a good destination. If you continue another mile or so, the amount of wading increases.

Small trout can be found in some of the pools along here, but there are very few "keepers." You may also notice the round tube-like structures made of sand which are so common on rocks in the water. These are the effective camouflage of the caddis fly larvae.

A hike of 3.0–3.5 miles in from the lodge makes a nice one-day outing. No camping or fires are permitted in West Fork.

Return by the same route.

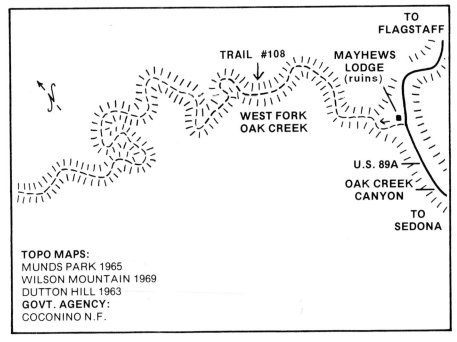

TOPO MAPS:
MUNDS PARK 1965
WILSON MOUNTAIN 1969
DUTTON HILL 1963
GOVT. AGENCY:
COCONINO N.F.

44 — WILSON MOUNTAIN TANK

Round trip 11.2 miles
All day, allow 8 hours
Approx. elevations 4,600–6,900
Season May through October

Among the attributes of this hike are beautiful views of the San Francisco Peaks and parts of Oak Creek Canyon.

From the junction of State 179 and U.S. 89A in Sedona, drive north on 89A for 1.8 miles to parking at the north of Midgley Bridge. The Forest Service requests that you do not park directly in front of the gate, thereby blocking access. The trailhead for F.S. Trail #10 is on the lefthand side of the road, and is directly beside a rock with a brass plaque commemorating Mr. Richard Wilson, an early settler in the region.

The trail starts with a steep pull up the hill, and after passing through an area of junipers, agaves, sumacs, shrub live oaks, manzanitas, pinyons and prickly pears, you will reach more level terrain.

The trail is not so steep along here but then switchbacks steeply to the mesa rim. Shade is available most of the way, but it can still be very hot during the warmer summer months.

From the rim, the trail continues a little less than a mile to a small saddle. Just before reaching that saddle, the North Wilson Trail, #123, intersects from the east. Wilson Mountain is not very far north of the saddle and there is a fairly good path all the way to the north edge of the summit. You may wish to continue a little over a mile from the saddle to Wilson Mountain Tank. Follow blazes and cairns carefully. The route is through a ponderosa pine forest with many open areas that afford opportunities to observe wildlife. The tank is small and shallow.

Wilson Mountain and Wilson Canyon were named for Richard Wilson who was killed by a bear in Wilson Canyon about 1885. The trail originated from local ranchers running herds of horses up the mountainside to graze.

Return by the same route.

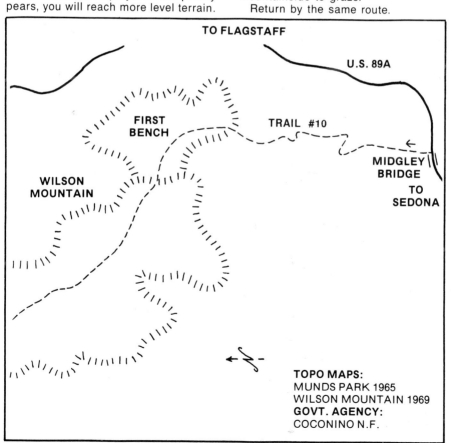

TO FLAGSTAFF

U.S. 89A

FIRST BENCH

TRAIL #10

WILSON MOUNTAIN

MIDGLEY BRIDGE

TO SEDONA

TOPO MAPS:
MUNDS PARK 1965
WILSON MOUNTAIN 1969
GOVT. AGENCY:
COCONINO N.F.

– VULTEE ARCH

ound trip 4 miles
?art day, allow 3 hours
Approx. elevations 4,800–5,400
Season April through October

This small but unique arch is named after Gerald Vultee and his wife Sylvia who were killed in a plane crash in this area in 1938. It is situated amid some of Arizona's finest scenery, and this is one of the choicest of short hikes.

From the junction of State 179 and U.S. 89A in Sedona, head west on 89A for 3.2 miles and turn right onto Dry Creek Road, F.S. 152. Proceed about 2 miles, then turn right onto F.S. 152 and continue for 4.3 miles to a parking area. The first part of the hike follows an old road to the start of the trail, which is F.S. Trail #22.

The trail heads gradually up Sterling Canyon. It crosses and recrosses a usually dry creekbed that winds through a pygmy forest of juniper against a backdrop of red canyon walls. About 0.75 mile in, there are tall, white sandstone cliffs on the right with Douglas first growing in the clefts.

The trail ends in an area of sandstone benches. There is a memorial plaque here, and the flat-topped arch is across the canyon. Please admire it from a respectful distance.

Return is by the same route.

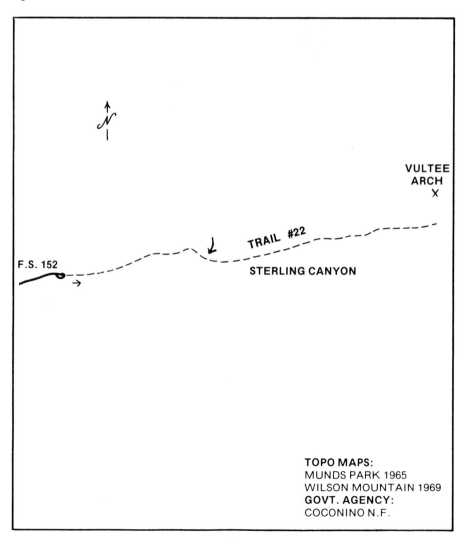

VULTEE
ARCH
X

TRAIL #22

F.S. 152

STERLING CANYON

TOPO MAPS:
MUNDS PARK 1965
WILSON MOUNTAIN 1969
GOVT. AGENCY:
COCONINO N.F.

46 — KENDRICK PEAK

Round trip 8 miles
Full day, allow 8 hours
Approx. elevations 7,980–10,400
Season late June through September

This hike starts out on a fire road but develops into an excellent hiking trail. There are some fine views from the lookout tower on the top.

From the junction of I-40 and I-17 near Flagstaff, head west about 10 miles on I-40, then go right on Transwestern. Proceed 0.25 mile and turn left (west) onto the frontage road paralleling I-40. Continue 1.1 miles on this frontage road, then turn to the right (north) on F.S. 171. Continue on this road for 11.5 miles to F.S. 171A. Take 171A to the right for 0.75 mile to the trailhead at the end of the road.

Pass through the gate at the parking area and hike up the road. This is F.S. Trail #22. It switchbacks steadily up through the woods and sunwashed meadows of bracken fern and wildflowers. The lower reaches of the hike are through ponderosa pine forest that has been thinned.

At about 1.25 miles, the road gives way to a foot trail. The route is entirely uphill and consists mainly of switchbacks. There are fir trees and aspen groves at the higher elevations, and numerous grasshoppers make the air crackle in late summer.

As the trail climbs, there are some good views of older cinder cones below, and the view from the lookout is an interesting confirmation of the volcanic history of the region. Keep an eye out for golden-mantled ground squirrels near the lookout tower at the summit. They resemble the chipmunks but are larger and have a stockier build.

Return is by the same route.

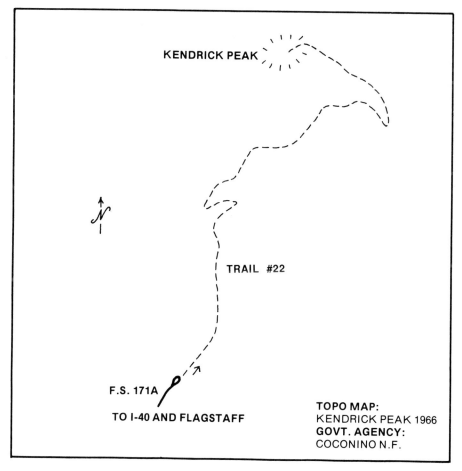

KENDRICK PEAK

TRAIL #22

F.S. 171A

TO I-40 AND FLAGSTAFF

TOPO MAP:
KENDRICK PEAK 1966
GOVT. AGENCY:
COCONINO N.F.

47 — MOUNT HUMPHREYS

Round Trip 7.5 miles
All day, allow ten hours
Approx. elevations 9,400-12,600
Season late June through September

At 12,670 feet, the eroded volcanic cone of Mount Humphreys is the highest point in Arizona. Nearby Mount Agassiz, at 12,400 feet, is the second highest. This limited area of the San Francisco Peaks is the only place in Arizona where alpine conditions exist. It is a long, steep hike, at high elevations, and only the very hardy hiker should attempt it. Temperatures are often cold and winds strong. A nice day in the morning, at the base, could turn into severe storm conditions later in the day, near the summit. Be certain you are familiar with the prevention, symptoms and treatment of hypothermia.

To get to the trailhead, proceed northwest on U.S. 180 7.2 miles from Flagstaff to the Arizona Snowbowl turnoff. Turn right, and drive 7.3 miles to the ski area parking lot. Walk past the ski lodge and up some steps, continuing along the wide ski run swath (Forest Service Trail #104). The ski lift will be to the right, and the lower portion of the route follows the ski swath, climbing steeply and steadily through a forest of quaking aspen and Engelmann spruce. As the elevation increases, some bristlecone pines will also be encountered.

After an arduous climb, the trail branches on the ridge connecting Mount Agassiz and Mount Humphreys. From there, the views are spectacular. Be careful, along the way, not to dislodge loose rocks which could cause you to fall or injure someone.

Trail #102 goes to the right and climbs Mount Agassiz. The views from Mount Agassiz are exceeded only by those from Humphreys. If time and weather permit, the hiker should consider taking both trails #102 and #104 for maximum enjoyment of the scenery. Trail #104 proceeds left, along the ridge, to the summit of Humphreys. Mount Humphreys is the somewhat higher point connected to Agassiz by a ridge. WARNING: There are places, expecially on the righthand side of the ridge, where there are steep cliffs. Patches of snow remain into July, and violent electrical storms sometimes occur on these high peaks.

Along the ridge, there are a few alpine plants and bristlecones that manage to exist. There are trails of use that come and go. The summit of Mount Humphreys is at 4.2 miles At the top there is a cairn and a summit register. The view is of hundreds of square miles of land, including Oak Creek Canyon, the Grand Canyon and Kendrick Peak.

Return is by the same route. Many hikers short-cut down the side of Humphreys to the snowbowl, but footing is often unstable so that, for safety reasons, we can't recommend short-cutting. The practice has already resulted in considerable erosion.

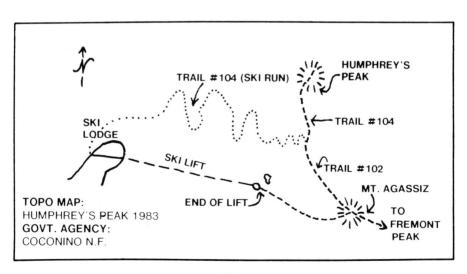

TRAIL #104 (SKI RUN)

HUMPHREY'S PEAK

SKI LODGE

SKI LIFT

TRAIL #104

END OF LIFT

TRAIL #102

MT. AGASSIZ

TO FREMONT PEAK

TOPO MAP:
HUMPHREY'S PEAK 1983
GOVT. AGENCY:
COCONINO N.F.

48 — NORTH KAIBAB

Round trip 28 miles
Backpack, allow 3 days
Approx. elevations 8,200-2,400
Season June through August

The North Rim is over a thousand feet higher than the South Rim and is entirely snowed in during the winter. This trail must be hiked during the summertime, and a camping permit must be obtained well in advance of your trip. Use is regulated, and many dates are booked ahead. It is a steep, rugged hike--often hot-- from the North Rim to the Colorado River some 14 miles down the trail. Allow at least twice as much time for the return trip as the trip down, and carry plenty of water.

From Jacob Lake, head south to Grand Canyon National Park. The turnoff to the Kaibab Trail parking area is just off the main road and is marked by a sign.

Aspens, ponderosa pines, Douglas firs and Gambel's oaks grow near the top of the trail. For the first several miles, the route is fairly steep and executes numerous switchbacks. Before reaching Roaring Springs, there are several places where the trail is narrow with sheer drops off the side.

Tremendous amounts of water gush from the side of the cliff at Roaring Springs, making this a good place for a rest stop. The steep grade slacks off between Roaring Springs and Cottonwood Camp, and there are far fewer switchbacks. Juniper, manzanita and pinyon are now common, and part of the route is very close to the creek.

Cottonwood Camp has a few picnic tables and campsites, but there is little shade, and it is an area that can be very hot at times.

The trail continues downhill from Cottonwood Camp for a gradual 1.8 miles to a short side trail going to Ribbon Falls. A sixty-foot travertine formation has developed at the base of the falls. The formation is delicate and should be observed only from a distance.

From the Ribbon Falls junction, the main trail descends more or less gradually for another 5.5 miles to Phantom Ranch and then to Bright Angel Campground which is just below the ranch. The last stretch is entirely along Bright Angel Creek (do not drink from it).

It is possible to hike out via the South Kaibab Trail (Hike 49) or the Bright Angel Trail (Hike 50), but be sure you have made transportation arrangements beforehand. Because of its steepness and exposure, the South Kaibab is not recommended for ascent in summer.

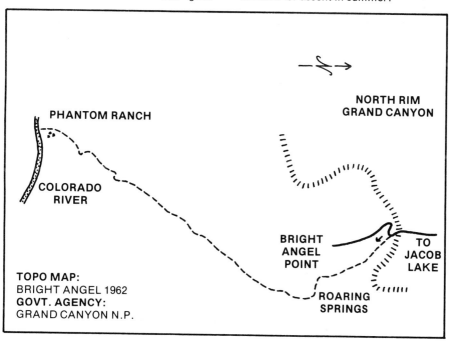

PHANTOM RANCH

COLORADO RIVER

NORTH RIM GRAND CANYON

BRIGHT ANGEL POINT

TO JACOB LAKE

ROARING SPRINGS

TOPO MAP:
BRIGHT ANGEL 1962
GOVT. AGENCY:
GRAND CANYON N.P.

49 — SOUTH KAIBAB

Round trip 14.6 miles
Backpack
Approx. elevations 7,200-2,400
Season all year except after storms

The South Kaibab Trail is an exciting route into the Grand Canyon--a veritable lesson in geology as it descends through the younger rock at the rim to the ancient rock near the river. The precipitous grade and exposure provide breathtaking views, but steepness and lack of shade make for a tortuous ascent during summer. There is no "easy" route out of the canyon, but if you hike down the South Kaibab in hot weather, it is recommended that you return via the longer but less arduous Bright Angel Trail. The two trails are some distance apart at the canyon rim, so arrange transportation between them before starting out.

Keep in mind that you must have a permit to backpack and camp in the canyon. The permit should be obtained well in advance of your trip because use is limited and many dates are booked ahead.

The trailhead is reached by turning east from U.S. 64-180 and proceeding on East Rim Drive for 1.1 miles to Yaki Point, then proceeding left for 0.5 mile to parking.

The trail descends to Cedar Ridge, a distance of 1.4 miles and a logical destination for day hikers. This point is 1,500 feet below the canyon rim in an area of interesting fossils and a display of fossilized ferns. There are good views from here, and the relatively flat Tonto Plateau can be seen far below.

Beyond Cedar Ridge the grade is more gradual for a time, and there are fewer switchbacks. The inner canyon is not yet visible, but the trailside geology is changing continuously, as are the views. The trail between the ridge and the Tonto Plateau offers one of the finest hiking experiences in the world. From some places you can see more than a mile of trail blasted out of the rock and as many as five or six switchbacks directly below. Mule trains often use this trail, and they have the right of way. Should you meet one, move to a safe place beside the trail to allow clearance.

Near the fourth mile the trail crosses the Tonto Plateau which is open and somewhat barren except for blackbrush. From the "Tip Off," just before the trail drops into the inner canyon, the Colorado River can be heard and seen far below.

The trail joins the River Trail near the canyon bottom, then crosses the Colorado via the Kaibab suspension bridge. Bright Angel Campground is located a short distance beyond the bridge, near the confluence of Bright Angel Creek and the river. Phantom Ranch is a short distance beyond the campground.

The round trip mileage given above is for return via the same route; however, the Bright Angel Trail (Hike 50) is recommended for a less strenuous ascent.

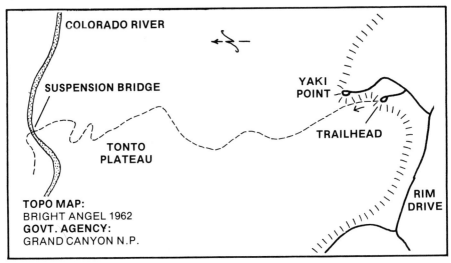

COLORADO RIVER

SUSPENSION BRIDGE

TONTO PLATEAU

YAKI POINT

TRAILHEAD

RIM DRIVE

TOPO MAP:
BRIGHT ANGEL 1962
GOVT. AGENCY:
GRAND CANYON N.P.

50 — BRIGHT ANGEL

Round trip 20.6 miles
Backpack
Approx. elevations 6,900-2,400
Season all year except after storms

This is a long, steep, rugged hike which follows the Bright Angel Fault into the Grand Canyon. It was used for centuries by Indians and later by prospectors who widened it. At one time a toll was charged to use it.

The trail is now maintained by the National Park Service. You must have a permit if you are going to backpack and camp in the canyon. This permit should be obtained well in advance of your trip as many dates are already booked and numbers are limited. If you plan to return by a different trail, be sure to arrange transportation before setting out.

The first 4.4 miles brings you through two man-made tunnels and down a series of steep switchbacks to Indian Gardens, an oasis shaded by cottonwoods which can be seen from the rim. Centuries ago, Indians raised crops here. Now it is the site of a pump station that lifts water which comes from near the North Rim up to the South Rim. This is a good turn-around point for day hikers. Plan on taking at least twice as long going up as you did coming down. Whether you are turning around or continuing down, be sure your canteens are full.

From Indian Gardens there is a 1.4-mile side trip across the Tonto Plateau to Plateau Point. You can look down into the inner gorge of the canyon from here.

Continue downhill from Indian Gardens for another 3.1 miles on the Bright Angel Trail. Part of the route is along Garden Creek, and the trail is fairly steep in places. Turn to the right when you reach the River Trail. This trail is relatively level as it more or less parallels the Colorado River below. Do not attempt to swim in the river.

Cross the suspension bridge and continue to Bright Angel Campground. From here it is possible to hike out via the South Kaibab Trail (Hike 49) or the North Kaibab Trail (Hike 48) if you have made transportation arrangements beforehand. Keep in mind that the North Kaibab Trail comes out on the North Rim and is closed in winter and that the South Kaibab Trail is not recommended for ascent in summer because of its steepness and exposure.

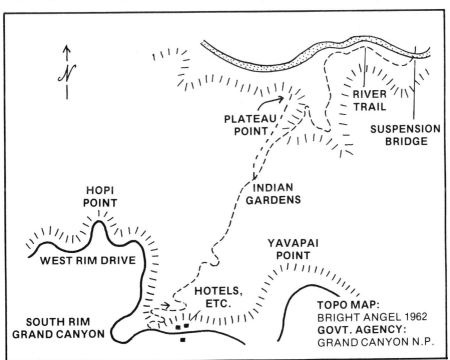

Sedona/Oak Creek Canyon Area

Douglas fir forest

Oak Creek Canyon

Grand Canyon

South Kaibab Trail in the Grand Canyon

Suspension Bridge at Bottom of Grand Canyon

Mile and a half house, Bright Angel Trail

Ascending Bright Angel Trail

Hedge Hog Cactus Blossoms

Heart of Rocks in the Chiricahuas

THE ARIZONA TRAIL

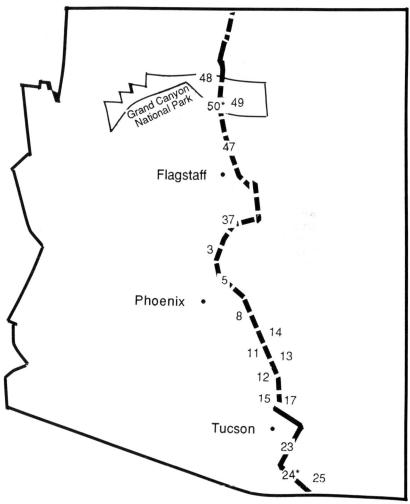

Grand Canyon National Park

48

50* 49

47

Flagstaff •

37

3

5

Phoenix •

8

14

11 13

12

15 17

Tucson •

23

24* 25

Completed segments of the Arizona Trail.
Projected Arizona Trail.
Numbers refer to hikes in this book that will be on or near the Arizona Trail.
* These hikes are included in the Arizona Trail.

Some day soon, hikers and equestrians will be able to start at the Utah-Arizona border and trek the whole north-south expanse of Arizona to the Mexican border. The state and national agencies within the state are cooperating on a massive adventure that will take hikers through National Forests, through desert regions, and over mountain peaks, with pauses at many of Arizona's lakes and streams. Part of the trail will lead across the Grand Canyon.

So far, 100 miles of the projected 700 mile trail have been dedicated, and descriptions are available for Kaibab Plateau Trail, Central Segment (Jacob Lake to Telephone

Hill), Kaibab Plateau Trail, Southern Segment (Telephone Hill to Grand Canyon National Park), Huachuca Mountain Passage (Coronado National Memorial to Parker Canyon Lake), Rincon Mountain Passage (Miller Creek to Italian Spring), and Santa Catalina Mountain Passage (Molino Basin to Oracle State Park). Hikers of these segments follow historic trails including one of the routes of the explorer Coronado.

Information about these hikes can be obtained from Arizona Trail Coordinator, Kaibab National Forest, 800 South Sixth Street, Williams, Arizona, 86046. Kaibab National Forest is just one of the national forest service agencies involved in the Arizona Trail project. 75% of the trail will pass through forest service administered land. 95% of the trail will pass through federal, state, or local government administered territory. It is a massive undertaking, much of it by volunteers from the Sierra Club and many hiking clubs. These aides will assist the national park services in the Sierra Vista, Nogales, Santa Catalina, Globe, Mesa, Tonto Basin, Cave Creek, Payson, Blue Ridge, Mormon Lake, Peaks, Tusayan and North Kaibab Ranger Districts. Also involved are the Arizona State Parks Trail Coordinator, Arizona Hiking and Equestrian Trail Committee, the National Park Service, and the U. S. Bureau of Land Management. Private agencies can participate through the Adopt-a-Trail program. A handbook describing sponsoring opportunities can be obtained from the Arizona State Parks, Trail Coordinator, 800 W. Washington, Suite 415, Phoenix, AZ 85007.

Much of the new trail will be formed by refurbishing older trails and joining them to make a continuous path. So, you will find segments of the Arizona Trail included in hikes in *50 Hikes in Arizona*. Miller Peak (hike no. 24) lies in the Huachuca Mountain Passage area. North Kaibab and South Kaibab (hikes 48 and 49) are routes into the Grand Canyon where in the Kaibab Plateau region, and Bright Angel Trail (hike 50) will eventually be part of the new trail.

The forest service advises that, even though the trail crosses highways and streets in many places, hiking will often be under primitive conditions.

INDEX TO PLACE NAMES
BY PAGE NUMBER